VIRTUES &
THE VIRTUOUS

INSPIRING LESSONS AND INSIGHTS ABOUT
VIRTUE, VIRTUOSITY, AND THE
ESSENCE OF THE HUMAN SPIRIT

Volume I

Kathy –
Thanks for
your hospitality

Gene Ferrar

E. F. Ferraro

Virtues & the Virtuous

Inspiring Lessons and Insights about Virtue, Virtuosity, and the
Essence of the Human Spirit
Volume I

Publisher:
AuthorVista LLC™
P.O. Box 57, Pine, Colorado 80470
info@AuthorVista.com

International Standard Book Numbers:

ISBN-10: 0-93730901-X
ISBN-13: 978-0-937309-01-8 (Paperback)
ISBN-13: 978-0-937309-02-5 (Paperback, Large Print Edition)
ISBN-13: 978-0-937309-03-2 (eBook)

First Edition

The author can be reached at Gene.Ferraro@AuthorVista.com or via
the web at www.AuthorVista.com or follow him on Twitter at
twitter.com/AuthorVista and Facebook at www.facebook.com/
AuthorVista.

Research and editing by Michelle Christensen
Content layout and format by AuthorVista LLC
Cover design by AuthorVista LLC

DEDICATION

We have been told that God could not be everywhere, and
therefore in his infinite wisdom, created mothers. I think it is so.
Thus it is Nancy, both my mother and friend, whose love
and wisdom has never ceased to warm the hearts
and soothe the souls of her many children.
I am most grateful to be one of them.

The most virtuous have something within them, a spirit which is bold, wise, and fearless. The virtuous possess righteous principles, but are not perfect. For if you believe a person of virtue must be found perfect, you might as well deny the sun for it does not always shine.

CONTENTS

ACKNOWLEDGMENTS

First, I thank the teachers, professors, and instructors who gave of themselves and taught me to read, write, and better understand the world around me. Without their virtues of devotion, patience, and wisdom, this work would have never been possible, no less imagined. I am forever grateful to them and those who similarly taught and endowed them.

I also thank my wife, Shelley. As I researched, sat, and wrote days on end, she cared for our home, horses, pets, and family affairs. Though it may seem otherwise, the wife of a writer knows not an easy life.

Next, I thank my faithful research assistant, copy editor, and proof reader, Michelle Christensen. She worked tirelessly and kept me focused, on schedule, and constantly writing. She is a wonderful parent and wife who cared for her family as she helped care for me and my work.

And finally, I thank all those whose lives, stories, and virtuosity contributed to the content of this book. Without them and their inspiring human spirit, the pages that follow would be empty, as would our hearts. God bless them, one and all.

Preface

While I have made every effort to properly credit, cite, and acknowledge those whose material or quotes I have used, in numerous instances it was impossible. Where it was possible, I noted the identity of the likely or most probable source. However, where that was not possible or unresolvable conflicts arose, I noted the source of the material as simply *anonymous*. To those whom credit is due, I humbly apologize. If those who know the proper source inform me of such, I will gladly make the correction in the next edition.

Material which is not credited, or identified as anonymous, is mine. If by chance someone else was first to record those words, I again apologize. If informed of such, I will give credit where due in the next edition. My contact information can be found on the copyright page and in my afterword.

On a final note, the reader should know that this book was written so as to not require it be read cover to cover. It has been formatted so any reader, at any time, can merely open the book and begin to read and enjoy it. Useful are the true-life short stories which begin each chapter. You will also notice that I have added occasional endnotes to some of the stories. They are intended to provide additional details or insight not contained in the story itself.

So crack it open and dive in. I assure your enjoyment and promise your time will be well spent. Thank you and prepare to be *inspired*.

E.F. Ferraro
Pine, Colorado

INTRODUCTION

It has been said, all things occur for a reason and nothing is the result of coincidence. Whether you believe that or not, reflect on it, and momentarily accept it as true. If you put aside the conventional, (and often convenient), notion things just happen, it is possible to imagine that everything which occurs is somehow interconnected—nothing occurs by itself. By extension, the events of today are the result of those that occurred yesterday and yesterday is the product of all the yesterdays that preceded it. Small, even imperceptible changes to any initial condition can precipitate a chain of events that eventually lead to large-scale alterations, often of remarkable proportions. This is more than just a belief, it is an insight into our essence and purpose. According to Chaos Theory, it is the glue which binds the future to the past. Quaintly, it is called the *butterfly effect*.

So what of it and who should care? Well as it turns out this idea of one event affecting all those that follow is the footing on which the world's great religions rest and nearly all of our most admired virtues—self-discipline, compassion, personal responsibility, perseverance, honesty, hope, and charity—are grounded. Consider personal responsibility. Some of us accept it, others don't. Although it is to their detriment, those who reject it consider the acceptance of personal responsibility as a choice, often made for mere convenience. They behave with little regard for that which they say or do, or the outcomes their actions produce. However there are others who cherish personal responsibility. They innately recognize that every personal decision and its corresponding action has the potential to initiate a life-changing chain of events often of profound proportions. These individuals accept the notion that they are solely responsible for the decisions they make, even when they are faulty and the outcomes they produce are undesirable. They know how and when to accept responsibility. They recognize the importance of personal responsibility, and possess the humility to embrace it. Their reward is a fuller, more abundant life.

To God's delight the world is filled with such people. Though many of them are seemingly ordinary, they are all around us. They are wise, simple, and virtuous people. Their wisdom is capable of profoundly changing our perception of virtuosity and all of the collateral obligations which adhere to it.

This book is about some of these individuals. It is not, however, a tribute to their inspiration and spirit. It is about that which they offered our world and how they so innocently were able to change it. In the pages that follow we will explore some of the timeless bits of wisdom they and others have offered us. We will see how their insights can influence our lives, warm our hearts, and when needed, soothe a badly bruised soul. And while you will not recognize all of them by name, their contributions personify the essence of goodness and good behavior. Their experiences and observations serve as lessons in character and morality. Their stories should stimulate as well as inspire the humanity that resides in each of us—for they are butterflies and *we* are their beneficiaries.

Yesterday is history and tomorrow may well be a mystery, but it is never too late to be what you might have been. For that reason, today is a gift from God, which is why we so respectfully call it the Present.

iv

1 COURAGE

---

*Courage is not the absence of fear. It's not being completely
unafraid. Courage is having apprehension and hesitation.
Courage is living in spite of those things that scare us.
Courage is the faith that some things will change and others
never will. It is the belief that failure is not fatal, but to carry
on when it is almost certain.*

T hough I had never met him in person, Scott and I
became quick friends. At age 4, Scott was diagnosed
with myotubular myopathy, a rare form of
centronuclear myopathy, which causes profound loss of muscle
tone and a weakness of all skeletal muscles. The disease is
progressive and cruel. Common symptoms include drooping of
the upper eyelids, facial weakness, foot drop, blackouts, as well
as increasing weakness of the limbs and upper body. It is a disease
for which no treatment is available, and whose victims often die
young of unarrestable pulmonary complications.

Scott and I met through his father. Mike at the time was an
accomplished attorney and security expert. We were close
professional colleagues, and over the years we frequently had the
opportunity to do volunteer work together. Regardless of the

matter at hand, Mike always found time for his family. Rather quickly, I noticed his frequent communications with his son, Scott. Curious to know more, I questioned him about his son and their relationship. Without hesitation and almost matter of fact, Mike shared with me that his only son had myotubular myopathy. Mike told me that Scott's life in a wheelchair began in junior high school, and though he had periods of what appeared to be remission, Scott's condition was slowly and painfully deteriorating. Upon request, he introduced me to Scott via email.

Over a period of something less than a year, Scott and I exchanged many emails and discussed many topics. Though much younger than I, we had something very much in common, the love of cooking. I also learned of his profound love for life. In spite of his challenges (and he had many along with disappointing setbacks and periodic hospitalizations), his attitude was up-beat and his communications were positive and full of spirit. "You'd never know he was having a hard day," claimed Lisa Rosen, the Education Program Manager at the Rehabilitation Institute of Chicago, where he spent much of his time (as both a patient and volunteer). In spite of his difficulty speaking, "He's always telling jokes, making you laugh," she said. And that was Scott—the consummate joker, comedian, and motivator. So much so, to the staff and patients at RIC he became known as *Mr. Determinator*. Others noticed him as well. In 2011, the Muscular Dystrophy Association named Scott the recipient of its Robert Ross National Personal Achievement Award for 2012. With great disappointment and sadness to everyone who knew him, he passed away the day he received the letter informing him of the award.

It appeared to me, and many others, Scott lived life as if he had no disabilities or impairments. He behaved as if his disease, and the burden it imposed on him was merely an inconvenience. He lived life as many of us should—thankful and full of joy. To remind us of that, he closed each email he wrote with his own inspiration:

Spread smiles to everybody, everywhere, each and every day. Eat well, laugh often, live, and love life.

Scott B. Crane possessed many virtues, but among them it was his courage that was most revealing. He had a settled disposition to feel appropriate degrees of fear and confidence when facing all that challenged him. Though his pained and crippled body bound him to a wheelchair, he had the courage to spread smiles, laugh often, live, and love life.[1]

It takes more courage to reveal insecurities than to hide them, more strength to relate to people than to dominate them, more 'manhood' to abide by thought-out principles rather than blind reflex. Toughness is in the soul and spirit, not in muscles and an immature mind.
—*Alex Karras*

Courage is not the absence of fear, but rather the judgment that something else is more important than fear.
—*Ambrose Redmoon*

Life shrinks or expands in proportion
to one's courage.
—*Anais Nin*

One man with courage makes a majority.
—*President, Andrew Jackson*

We become brave by doing brave things.
—*Aristotle*

Nothing is impossible, the word itself
says 'I'm possible!'
—*Audrey Hepburn*

How few there are who have courage enough to
own their faults, or resolution
enough to mend them.
—*Benjamin Franklin*

Courage is contagious. When a brave man takes a
stand, the spines of others are often stiffened.
—*Billy Graham*

Mistakes are always forgivable, if one has the
courage to admit them.
—*Bruce Lee*

Courage is not living without fear. Courage is
being scared to death and doing the
right thing anyway.
—*Chae Richardson*

Courage is not limited to the battlefield or the
Indianapolis 500, or bravely catching a thief
in your house. The real tests of courage
are much quieter. They are the inner tests, like
remaining faithful when nobody's looking, like
enduring pain when the room is empty, like
standing alone when you're misunderstood.
—*Charles Swindoll*

Faced with what is right, to leave it undone
shows a lack of courage.
—*Confucius*

The most courageous act is still to think
for yourself. Aloud.
—*Coco Chanel*

Courage is not simply one of the virtues, but the
[essence] of every virtue at its testing point.
—*C.S. Lewis*

Courage is as often the outcome of despair as of
hope; in the one case we have nothing to lose, in
the other everything to gain.
—*Diane de Poitiers*

It takes courage to grow up and become
who you really are.
—*E.E. Cummings*

Courage is doing what you're afraid to do. There
can be no courage unless you're scared.
—*Eddie Rickenbacker*

The encouraging thing is that every time you
meet a situation, though you may think at the
time it is an impossibility and you go through the
tortures of the damned, once you have met it and
lived through it you find that forever after you
are freer than you ever were before.
—*First Lady Eleanor Roosevelt*

Perfect courage means doing unwitnessed what
he would be capable of with the
world looking on.
—*Francois de La Rouchefoucauld*

Courage is fear holding on a minute longer.
—*General George S. Patton*

I wanted you to see what real courage is, instead
of getting the idea that courage is a man with a
gun in his hand. It's when you know you're licked
before you begin but you begin anyway and you

see it through no matter what. You rarely win,
but sometimes you do.
—*Harper Lee*

Creativity takes courage.
—*Henri Matisse*

Unless you have courage, a courage that keeps
you going, always going, no matter what happens,
there is no certainty of success.
It is really an endurance race.
—*Henry Ford*

Fall down seven times, get up eight.
—*Japanese Proverb*

Courage and perseverance have a magic talisman,
before which difficulties
and obstacles vanish into air.
—*President, John Adams*

A great leader's courage to fulfill his vision comes
from passion, not position.
—*John Maxwell*

There is no living thing that is not afraid when it
faces danger. The true courage is in
facing danger when you are afraid.
—*L. Frank Baum*

When we are afraid we ought not to occupy
ourselves with endeavoring to prove that there is
no danger, but in strengthening ourselves to go
on in spite of the danger.
—*Mark Rutherford*

It is curious that physical courage should
be so common in the world and
moral courage so rare.
—*Mark Twain*

Courage doesn't always roar. Sometimes courage
is the little voice at the end of the day that says
'I'll try again tomorrow.'
—*Mary Anne Radmacher*

Courage is the most important of all the virtues,
because without courage you can't practice any
other virtue consistently. You can practice
any virtue erratically, but [none]
consistently without courage.
—*Maya Angelou*

He who is not courageous enough to take risks
will accomplish nothing in life.
—*Muhammad Ali*

The brave man is not he who does not feel afraid,
but he who conquers that fear.
—*Nelson Mandela*

Above all, be the heroine of your
life, not the victim.
—*Nora Ephron*

Whatever you do, you need courage. Whatever
course you decide upon, there is always someone
to tell you that you are wrong. There are always
difficulties arising that tempt you to believe your
critics are right. To map out a course of action
and follow it to an end requires some of
the same courage a soldier needs.
—*Ralph Waldo Emerson*

Keep your fears to yourself, but share
your courage with others.
—*Robert Lewis Stevenson*

Extraordinary people survive under the most
terrible circumstances and they become more
extraordinary because of it.
—*Robertson Davies*

Courage is like a muscle.
We strengthen it with use.
—*Ruth Gordon*

Have the courage to follow your heart and
intuition. They somehow already know
what you truly want to become.
—*Steve Jobs*

Sometimes you don't realize your own strength
until you come face to face with
your greatest weakness.
—*Susan Gale*

Courage is the discovery that you may not win,
and trying when you know you can lose.
—*Thomas Krause*

Healing takes courage and we all have courage,
even if we have to dig a little to find it.
—*Tori Amos*

Anything is possible,
the impossible just takes longer.
—*U.S. Marine Corps proverb*

Often the test of courage is not to die but to live.
—*Vittorio Alfiere*

All our dreams can come true if we have the
courage to pursue them.
—*Walt Disney*

Courage is what it takes to stand up and speak;
courage is also what it takes to
sit down and listen.
—*Sir Winston Churchill*

Courage is knowing that you're beaten
and forging ahead anyway.
—*Zach Wahls*

Anonymously…

Courage is the display of grace
when under pressure.

True strength is keeping everything together
when everyone expects you to fall apart.

Anyone can give up, it's the easiest thing in the
world to do, but to keep it together when
everyone else would understand if you fell apart,
that's true strength.

Courage involves the making of errors and
mistakes, for they are the necessary steps in the
learning process; once they have served their
purpose, those errors and mistakes should be
forgotten and not repeated.

And from the author…

Courageous is to think aloud when
no else is talking.

Courage isn't something most of us are born with. It must be found, nurtured, and given the opportunity to develop. Doing is the stimulant and results are the reward.

We never know how strong we are until being strong is our only choice.

Courage is not limited to the battlefield or fighting for that which is right. The real test of courage is much quieter. It is doing right when no one is looking, remaining faithful when alone, enduring pain when there is no hope, and standing tall in the face of your enemy and his kind.

It appears on occasion that moderation has been called a virtue so as to limit the courage of others, and console the undistinguished and their lack of merit.

The courageous always seem to find the time to check their fear at the door.

There is no sane being that is not afraid when facing danger. The truly courageous face danger even when afraid.

We must do the things we think we cannot; for to
do otherwise is the epitome of failure.

The courageous never see themselves as
courageous, they simply are.

*"You will be courageous by doing courageous things," said the lioness to
her cub. To which the young cub replied, "I will not disappoint you for I
fear not the unknown but wish only the chance to demonstrate I am
brave." "Ah," said the lioness, "you need not demonstrate your bravery
to anyone—you must only reveal it to yourself."*

---

[1] Before his death, with the assistance of others, Scott Crane founded *In
Chef's Hands*, a nonprofit dedicated to "food therapy for the soul." The
organization provides educational experience for special needs individuals
who have a passion for food and cooking. AuthorVista proudly supports it
by donating a portion of the revenue from every book it sells to this worthy
organization. To learn more go to its website found at
www.InChefsHands.org.

2 PERSEVERANCE

Few things can take the place of perseverance. Talent will not;
nothing is more common than unsuccessful people with talent.
Genius will not; the world is full of educated derelicts, nor
will beauty or brawn. Perseverance and its companion
determination, together determine our fate. Combined they are
omnipotent and when seized, they can be ours forever.

From the start, little Stevland was not a typical child. Born six weeks premature to Calvin and Lula Mae, his little body was placed into a warm, oxygen-rich incubator. Little did anyone know, he would become blind before his tiny eyes were able to open.[2]

At the age of four, his mother left his father and their home in Saginaw, Michigan, and moved with the children to a small apartment on Hastings Street in Detroit. It was an area once known to the French explorers as, *Fond Noir*, or as Lula Mae Hardaway's neighbors knew it, Black Bottom.[3] Though it bustled, it was poor and in decline. To start afresh, Lula Mae changed the family name to Morris.

Life was difficult for little Stevland. Because of his shyness he had few friends and struggled in school. But of all the things he might have since forgotten, or remembers of it, one woman stood out and changed his life *and ours*, forever.

You see, Mrs. Beneduci was an elementary-school teacher with enormous compassion. She was also very wise. She knew words alone could not inspire a fidgety nine-year-old. With the unwitting aid of a little gray mouse she seized upon an opportunity that changed the life of that little boy and generations to come.

Mrs. Beneduci called her class to order. "Settle down…today we are going to learn about history," she told them. "It's a lovely day, and I know you'd rather play outside. But if you learn nothing in life, all you will ever know is how to play." Though his peers squirmed and giggled, Stevland sat silent.

"OK, who was Abraham Lincoln," she asked. One of her students replied, "He had a beard!" The class erupted in laughter.

"Steve Morris…same question." To which Stevland replied without hesitation, "He was the sixteenth President of the United States." The sudden silence became deafening. One after another, he answered her questions correctly. His problem was not the answers to the questions she thought, he knew them all; it was his inability to realize the gift he possessed.

Suddenly, Ms. Beneduci stopped her rapid fire questions and cried, "What's that…who's making that awful scratching noise?" Adding without thought, "It sounds like a mouse!"

A sudden uproar, came over the class. Some screamed, others

stood upon their chairs. "Calm please, I'm sorry, it's nothing to get excited about," said the teacher, flapping her arms as if to suppress their fear. "Steve will you help me find the mouse?" she asked.

"OK," he replied, and the room again became silent. Cocking his head and turning slowly, he pointed to the wastebasket he could not see. "He's right over there!—I can hear him, he's in the basket," he softly said.

And so he was, hiding beneath the wastepaper in a basket across the room, rustled a frightened tiny gray mouse. Discovered by a boy without sight, without searching, relying only on his extraordinary sense of hearing. A sense he had honed from birth in order to compensate for what his eyes had denied him.

From that moment forward, the compassionate Ms. Constance S. Beneduci would continue to encourage the talent of young Stevland. In doing so, he acquired an ear for music and soon became a popular singer and accomplished musician *before* the age of 12.[4] It was through perseverance and a profound dedication to music he learned to play the piano, synthesizer, harmonica, congas, drums, bass guitar, bongos, organ, melodica, and clavinet. Today, we know that little boy as Stevie Wonder.

Loved the world over, Stevie Wonder has since recorded more than 30 U.S. top ten hits and received 22 Grammy Awards, the most ever awarded to a male solo artist. He has sold over 100 million albums and singles, making him one of the top 60 best-selling music artists to have ever lived. But it was his perseverance to overcome the disability of blindness, and the compassion of a single teacher, that enabled little Stevland Morris to win our hearts and soothe our ears.[5]

Rivers know this: there is no hurry.
We shall get there some day.
—*A.A. Milne*

Success is a function of persistence and
doggedness and the willingness to work hard for
twenty-two minutes to make sense of
something that most people would
give up on after thirty seconds.
—*Alan Schoenfeld*

There are two ways of attaining an important end;
force and perseverance; the silent power of the
latter grows irresistible with time.
—*Anne Sophie Swetchine*

It's hard to beat the person that never gives up.
—*Babe Ruth*

Through perseverance many people win success
out of what seemed destined to be certain failure.
—*Benjamin Disraeli*

Remember, you only have to
succeed the last time.
—*Brian Tracy*

I think a hero is an ordinary individual who finds
the strength to persevere and endure in spite of
overwhelming obstacles.
—*Christopher Reeve*

Don't be afraid to give your best to what
seemingly are small jobs. Every time you conquer
one it makes you that much stronger.
If you do the little jobs well, the big ones will
tend to take care of themselves.
—*Dale Carnegie*

By gnawing through a dike,
even a rat may drown a nation.
—*Edmund Burke*

The practice of perseverance is the discipline
of the noblest virtues. To run well, we must run
to the end. It is not the fighting but the
conquering that gives a hero his title to renown.
—*Elias Lyman Magoon*

Failure after long perseverance is much
grander than never to have a striving
good enough to be called a failure.
—*George Eliot*

You go on. You set one foot in front of the
other, and if a thin voice cries out, somewhere

behind you, you pretend not to hear it,
and keep going.
—*Geraldine Brooks*

When you get into a tight place and everything
goes against you, till it seems as though you could
not hold on a minute longer, never give
up then, for that is just the place
and time that the tide will turn.
—*Harriet Beecher Stowe*

Perseverance is a great element of success. If you
only knock long enough and loud enough at the
gate, you are sure to wake up somebody.
—*Henry Wadsworth Longfellow*

The difference between perseverance and
obstinacy is that one often comes from a strong
will, and the other from a strong won't.
—*Henry Ward Beecher*

It is not enough to begin; continuance is
necessary. Mere enrollment will not make one a
scholar; the pupil must continue in the school
through the long course, until he masters every
branch. Success depends upon staying power.
The reason for failure in most cases
is lack of perseverance.
—*James Russell Miller*

I do not think that there is any other quality so
essential to success of any kind as
the quality of perseverance.
It overcomes almost everything,
even nature.
—*John D. Rockefeller*

Patience and perseverance have a magical effect
before which difficulties disappear
and obstacles vanish.
—*President, John Quincy Adams*

You've got to say, 'I think that if I keep working
at this and want it badly enough I can have it.'
It's called perseverance.
—*Lee Iacocca*

The drops of rain make a hole in the stone not by
violence but by oft falling.
—*Lucretius*

Life is not easy for any of us. But what of that?
We must have perseverance and above all
confidence in ourselves. We must believe that we
are gifted for something and that this
thing must be attained.
—*Marie Curie*

If you can't fly then run, if you can't run then
walk, if you can't walk then crawl, but whatever

you do you have to keep moving forward.
—*Martin Luther King, Jr.*

Determination and perseverance move the world;
thinking that others will do
it for you is a sure way to fail.
—*Marva Collins*

You may encounter many defeats, but you must
not be defeated. In fact, it may be necessary to
encounter defeats, so you can know who you are,
what you can rise from,
how you can still come out of it.
—*Maya Angelou*

I hated every minute of training, but I said,
'Don't quit. Suffer now and live the rest
of your life as a champion.'
—*Muhammad Ali*

What we do not see, what most of us never
suspect of existing, is the silent but irresistible
power which comes to the rescue of those who
fight on in the face of discouragement.
—*Napoleon Hill*

It always seems impossible until it's done.
—*Nelson Mandela*

So long as there is breath in me, that long I will
persist. For now I know one of the
greatest principles on success; if I persist
long enough I will win.
—*Og Mandino*

There is genius in persistence. It conquers all
opposers. It gives confidence. It annihilates
obstacles. Everybody believes in a determined
man. People know that when he undertakes a
thing, the battle is half won, for his rule is to
accomplish whatever he sets out to do.
—*Orison Swett Marden*

Perseverance is more prevailing than violence;
and many things which cannot be overcome
when they are together, yield themselves up
when taken little by little.
—*Plutarch*

The brick walls are there for a reason. The brick
walls are not there to keep us out. The brick walls
are there to give us a chance to show how badly
we want something. Because the brick walls are
there to stop the people who don't want it badly
enough. They're there to stop the other people.
—*Randy Pausch*

Stubbornly persist, and you will find that the
limits of your stubbornness go well beyond the

stubbornness of your limits.
—*Robert Brault*

If I had to select one quality, one personal
characteristic that I regard as being most highly
correlated with success, whatever the field, I
would pick the trait of persistence.
—*Robert M. Devos*

Great works are performed not by strength,
but by perseverance.
—*Samuel Johnson*

Permanence, perseverance, and persistence in
spite of all obstacles, discouragements, and
impossibilities: It is this, that in all things
distinguishes the strong soul from the weak.
—*Thomas Carlyle*

Many of life's failures are people who did not
realize how close they were to
success when they gave up.
—*Thomas A. Edison*

With ordinary talent and extraordinary
perseverance, all things are attainable.
—*Thomas Foxwell Buxton*

The harder the conflict, the more glorious the
triumph. What we obtain too cheap, we esteem
too lightly; it is dearness only that gives
everything its value. I love the man that can smile
in trouble, that can gather strength from
distress and grow brave by reflection.
—*Thomas Paine*

I am not judged by the number of times I fail, but
by the number of times I succeed; and the
number of times I succeed is in direct proportion
to the number of times I fail and keep trying.
—*Tom Hopkins*

Perseverance is not a long race; it is many
short races one after the other.
—*Walter Elliot*

But the person who scored well on an SAT will
not necessarily be the best doctor or the best
lawyer or the best businessman. These tests do
not measure character, leadership,
creativity, perseverance.
—*William Julius Wilson*

Anonymously...

The greatest oak was once a little nut
that held its ground.

Remember that guy that gave up?
Neither does anyone else.

Many of the great achievements of the world
were accomplished by tired and discouraged men
who kept on working.

There is no telling how many miles you will have
to run while chasing a dream.

It is hard to say which came first, the dream or
perseverance? No matter, dreams without
perseverance, are just dreams.

And from the author…

A hero is an ordinary person who finds the
strength to persevere in spite of the
opposition and the consequences of failure.

Saints are sinners who kept on trying.

Strength and perseverance are often confused.
Our struggles develop our strength, our courage
develops our perseverance.

The harder I toil the luckier I seem to get.

If one's attitude determines their altitude, then
perseverance determines their speed.

Determination is doing something others have
determined not to do.

Only I can destroy my determination,
others can only strengthen it.

Strong souls are seared with scars.

Our perseverance is capable of
inspiring the uninspired.

We have not the power to control events, only
the power of our will to overcome them.

Play hard, drink wine, and get to work.

*Next to courage, perseverance, and faith, diamonds and pearls are the
rarest things God created. Maybe so, but without man's courage,
perseverance, and faith, diamond and pearls would have never been
discovered, or value placed upon them. The same cannot
be said about either, diamonds or pearls.*

---

[2] Premature birth can cause the blood vessels from the retina into the back of the eye to stop growing or grow abnormally. Scar tissue may develop and pull the retina loose from the inner surface of the eye. In severe cases, this can result in the retinas to detach, causing vision loss or complete blindness. Exposing the developing eye to too much oxygen is another cause. The condition today is called *retinopathy of prematurity* (ROP), and is very rare.

[3] The name Black Bottom was not a reference to the predominately black community it had become. The French had originally called it Fond Noir because of its once fertile soil. Also known as Paradise Valley, the area became known for its significant contribution to American music to include Blues, Big Band, and Jazz from the 1930s to the 1950s. Left in disrepair, the neighborhood was eventually demolished and replaced with Lafayette Park in the 1960s. Wikipedia, http://en.wikipedia.org/wiki/Stevie_Wonder, December 4, 2014.

[4] In 1961, at age 11, he sang his own composition, *Lonely Boy*, to Ronnie White of the Miracles. So impressed was White, he took Stevland and his mother to an audition at Motown Records, where CEO Berry Gordy immediately signed little Stevland to Motown's Tamla label. But before signing, producer Clarence Paul renamed Stevland Morris, *Little Stevie Wonder*. Ibid.

[5] In lasting honor of his mother, Stevie Wonder retains the legal surname, Morris, and it is with this name, he signs all legal documents.

3 FAITH

Faith is the complete trust or confidence in someone or something. It is the belief in God, His power and His mercy. It is the ability to believe when no one else believes. Faith is the assurance of things hoped for and the conviction of things yet seen or realized. It is neither oppressive nor coercive, for it is an unshakable belief. Thus, through life we walk by faith, not by sight.

Ned was born in Boston on Oct. 7, 1931. The son of a marine architect and navy officer, he was raised to respect his parents, treat others with kindness, and love God. He was handsome, athletic, and smart. He graduated from the U.S. Naval Academy in 1954 and arrived in Vietnam in September 1967 aboard the nuclear powered carrier, the USS ENTERPRISE.

The ENTERPRISE had arrived on Yankee Station on December 2, 1965, and at the time, the largest warship ever built. She brought with her not only an imposing physical presence, but also a lethal complement of warplanes and advanced technology. By the end of her first week in hostile waters, the ENTERPRISE had set a record of 165 combat sorties in a single day. By the end of her first combat cruise, her planes and aircrews had flown over 13,000 combat missions. But the record had not been achieved without cost.

On March 17, 1968, Ned and his Bombardier/Navigator, Dale Doss, launched in their A6-A Intruder on a night, low-level strike into the heart of North Vietnam. After their departure they emitted their first radio transmission indicating that they were "feet dry" and over land, proceeding stealthily to their target, a rail yard just north of Hanoi. It would prove to be their final communication.

Undated U.S. Navy photograph of Ned beside his A6 Intruder.

The next day, Radio Hanoi announced the capture of Ned and his bombardier. Following what had begun as his 18th combat mission, suddenly he had become a prisoner of war.

Both Ned and Dale were transported to a filthy camp near the center of Hanoi, called by its prisoners, the *Hanoi Hilton*. There, Ned (like Dale and hundreds others), was beaten, tortured and held in solitary confinement. After 17 months he and Dale were reunited, and soon joined some of their fellow prisoners. For what seemed a lifetime, they sat, waited, and gave emotional support to one another. Then a miracle occurred.

Shortly before Christmas in 1970, Ned and 42 other American prisoners of war decided to break prison rules and hold a brief service in celebration of the birth of their savior. But their barbaric and inhumane guards stopped them. In their presence, Ned stepped forward and asked his emaciated fellow servicemen, "Are we really committed to having church Sunday? I want to know person by person." Fellow prisoner, Leo K. Thorsness, later recounted in a memoir, "When the 42nd man said yes, it was unanimous. At that instant, Ned knew he would end up in the torture cells."[6] The following Sunday, Ned stepped forward to lead a prayer session and was quickly hustled away by angry guards. The next four ranking officers did the same, one by one, they too, were taken away to be beaten. And then, Thorsness remembered, the sixth-ranking senior officer began, "Gentlemen, the Lord's Prayer—*Our Father*, who art in heaven, hallowed be thy name...And this time, we finished it." Realizing they were facing men who believed in a God they could only imagine, the humbled guards relented and no one was punished.

Lt. Commander Edwin A. Shuman III, known to his fellow comrades as Ned, remained incarcerated at the Hanoi Hilton for more than two additional years. But it was Ned, the downed navy pilot, a man of impeccable courage and unshakable faith, who had won the prisoners' privilege to collective prayer.[7]

It is better to believe than to disbelieve; in so
doing, you bring everything to
the realm of possibility.
—*Albert Einstein*

It is only with the heart that one can see rightly;
what is essential is invisible to the eye.
—*Antoine de Saint-Exupery*

Faith is different from proof; the latter is human,
the former is a gift from God.
—*Blaise Pascal*

Faith obliterates time, annihilates distance, and
brings future things at once into possession.
—*Charles Spurgeon*

Just because you can't see it doesn't mean it isn't
there. You can't see the future,
yet you know it will come; you can't see the air,
yet you continue to breathe.
—*Claire London*

Faith is not simply a patience that passively
suffers until the storm has past. Rather, is a spirit
that bears things with blazing serene hope.
—*Corazon Aquino*

If we become completely whole-hearted we will
have love for all people and will seek in each
person what is most holy, what God has inspired
in him or her. And only then will there be no
danger of softening or twisting our witness. Why?
Because the capacity of our faith will no longer
be narrow. If we are not broad-hearted, we have
not yet grasped the meaning of faith.
—*Eberhard Arnold*

Only with faith in something even greater than
our own determination can we take the
final seemingly impossible steps
forward to lasting change.
—*Edward Grinnan*

Faith is walking face-first and
full-speed into the dark.
—*Elizabeth Gilbert*

Absolute faith corrupts as absolutely
as absolute power.
—*Eric Hoffer*

Only the person who has faith in himself is able
to be faithful to others.
—*Erich Fromm*

Faith is not merely hope, and it must be more
than belief; faith is a knowing of the heart.
—*Rev. Floyd and M. Elaine Flake*

If you have abandoned one faith, do not abandon
all faith. There is always an alternative to the faith
we lose. Or is it the same faith
under another mask?
—*Graham Greene*

Faith, like sight is nothing apart from God. You
might as well shut your eyes and look inside, and
see whether you have sight as to look inside to
discover whether you have faith.
—*Hannah Whitall Smith*

I know that faith made my life possible and that
of many others like me... Reason hardly
warranted Anne Sullivan's attempt to transform a
little half-human, half-animal, deaf-blind child
into a complete human being. Neither science
nor philosophy had set such a goal, but faith, the
eye of love did. I did not know I had a soul. Then
the God in a wise heart drew me out of
nothingness with cords of human love and the
life belt of language, and lo, I found myself. In
my doubly shadowed world, faith gives me a
reason for trying to draw harmony out of a
marred instrument. Faith is not a cushion for me
to fall back upon; it is my working energy.
—*Helen Keller*

Back of every creation, supporting it like an arch, is
faith. Enthusiasm is nothing: it comes and goes.
But if one believes, then miracles occur.
—*Henry Miller*

Where faith is there is courage, there is fortitude,
there is steadfastness and strength…
Faith bestows that sublime courage that rises
superior to the troubles and disappointments of
life, that acknowledges no defeat except as a step
to victory; that is strong to endure, patient to wait,
and energetic to struggle…
Light up, then, the lamp of faith in your heart…
It will lead you safely through the mists of doubt
and the black darkness of despair;
along the narrow, thorny ways of sickness and
sorrow, and over the treacherous places of
temptation and uncertainty.
—*James Allen*

God has already done everything He's going to do.
The ball is now in your court. If you want success,
if you want wisdom, if you want to be prosperous
and healthy, you're going to have to do more
than meditate and believe; you must boldly
declare words of faith and victory over
yourself and your family.
—*Joel Osteen*

Out of suffering comes the serious mind; out of
salvation, the grateful heart; out of endurance,

fortitude; out of deliverance, faith.
—*John Ruskin*

Faith isn't the ability to believe long and far into
the misty future. It's simply taking God at His
word and taking the next step.
—*Joni Erickson Tada*

Faithless is he who says farewell
when the road darkens.
—J.R.R. Tolkien

Faith is a knowledge within the heart,
beyond the reach of proof.
—*Kahlil Gibran*

I claim to be an average man of less than average
ability. I have not the shadow of doubt that any
man or woman can achieve what I have, if he or
she would make the same effort and cultivate
the same hope and faith.
—*Mahatma Gandhi*

That's the thing about faith. If you don't have it
you can't understand it. And if you do,
no explanation is necessary.
—*Major Kira Nerys*

Sometimes your only available
transportation is a leap of faith.
—*Margaret Shepard*

Your belief determines your action and
your action determines your results,
but first you have to believe.
—*Mark Victor Hansen*

Faith is taking the first step even when you
don't see the whole staircase.
—*Martin Luther King, Jr.*

Faith moves mountains, but you have to keep
pushing while you are praying.
—*Mason Cooley*

If patience is worth anything, it must endure to
the end of time. And a living faith will last in the
midst of the blackest storm.
—*Mohandas Gandhi*

The antidote to frustration is a calm faith, not in
your own cleverness, or in hard toil,
but in God's guidance.
—*Norman Vincent Peale*

Faith...when you come to the edge of all the light
you have, and are about to step off into the

darkness of the unknown, faith is knowing one of
two things will happen: There will be something
solid to stand on, or you will be
taught how to fly.
—*Patrick Overton*

We are twice armed if we fight with faith.
—*Plato*

Faith is the bird that feels the light when
the dawn is still dark.
—*Rabindranath Tagore*

Our faith comes in moments... yet there is a
depth in those brief moments which constrains
us to ascribe more reality to them than
to all other experiences.
—*Ralph Waldo Emerson*

Faith is the spark that ignites the impossible and
causes it to become possible. When a person's
faith is activated, it sets in motion supernatural
power that enables that person to do what he
normally would never be able to do!
—*Rick Renner*

Faith is to believe what you do not see; the
reward of this faith is to see what you believe.
—*Saint Augustine*

You can do very little with faith, but you
can do nothing without it.
—*Samuel Butler*

Fear looks; faith jumps. Faith never fails to obtain
its object. If I leave you as I found you, I am not
God's channel. I am not here to entertain you,
but to get you to the place where
you can laugh at the impossible.
—*Smith Wigglesworth*

To believe only possibilities is not faith,
but merely philosophy.
—*Sir Thomas Browne*

Just as a small fire is extinguished by the storm
whereas a large fire is enhanced by it – likewise a
weak faith is weakened by predicament and
catastrophes whereas a strong faith is
strengthened by them.
—*Viktor Frankl*

May it not be that, just as we have to have faith in
Him, God has to have faith in us, and considering
the history of the human race so far, may it not
be that "faith" is even more difficult
for Him than it is for us?
—*W.H. Auden*

Faith is daring the soul to go beyond
what the eyes see.
—*William Newton Clark*

Without faith a man can do nothing;
with it all things are possible.
—*Sir William Osler*

Anonymously…

Faith is not without worry or care, but faith is fear
that has said a prayer.

Every tomorrow has two handles. We can take
hold of it by the handle of anxiety,
or by the handle of faith.

Faith isn't faith until it's all you're holding onto.

Fortunately, faith is not squandered on
the faithless.

Faith is believing in something when common
sense tells you not to.

Be patient with the faithful; sometimes
they're all you've got.

Faith makes things possible, not easy.

And from the author…

Faith is a wager, the bigger the bet, the
bigger the potential reward.

Don't worry about the future, just go as far as you
can and let faith do the rest.

Sometimes faith isn't enough, but complete
faith almost always is.

Faith is about trusting God,
even when it seems God is not listening.

A man of courage is a man of faith.

If fear is cultivated it becomes stronger, if faith is
cultivated it becomes strength.

Faith is passion without limits.

If you believe in God, God will believe in you.

God never made a promise *you* couldn't keep.

Robin once shrieked, "Holy strawberries Batman,
we're in a jam now," to which Batman replied,
"Have faith Robin, this joke is on the Joker."

When fear knocked, faith answered. And lo,
no one was there.

Have faith in God and let the Marines do the rest.

Be careful what you pray for, you might just
receive it when you least expect it.

Our Father who art in heaven, hallowed be thy name.
Thy kingdom come. Thy will be done on earth, as it is in heaven.
Give us this day our daily bread, and forgive us our trespasses, as we
forgive those who trespass against us, and lead us not into temptation,
but deliver us from evil.[8]

[6] Lt. Col. Thorsness, an Air Force pilot and recipient of the Medal of Honor for heroics on a mission in April 1967, wrote what he had witnessed in his memoir, *Surviving Hell: A POW's Journey* (2008), "I know I will never see a better example of pure raw [faith] or ever pray with a better sense of the meaning of the word."

[7] Lt. Cmd. Shuman was not without resentment. In a debriefing, following his repatriation he told his military interviewers that if it were not for the antiwar movement in the U.S. and celebrity sympathizers, the treatment of the U.S. prisoners held by the North Vietnamese would have been briefer and more civilized. He credited much of the mistreatment and torture he and other prisoners suffered to those who sympathized with the enemy.

[8] As found at http://www.vatican.va/archive/ccc_css/archive/catechism/p4s2.htm

4 FRIENDSHIP

A friend can be silent with us in a moment of despair or confusion. A friend can stay beside us in an hour of grief and bereavement. A friend can tolerate not knowing, not curing, not healing, and face with us the reality of our vulnerability and powerlessness. But only a forever friend is without envy and celebrates with us our joys and triumphs.

R ay once told me, "The best kind of friend is the kind you can share a porch swing, never say a word, and then walk away feeling like it was the best conversation you've ever had."[9] He also told me to, "Always be first to say hello; look other people in the eye; wear polished shoes; never cheat or be dishonest, learn to slow dance, and always buy your vegetables from a truck-farmer who advertises with a hand-lettered sign."

He was born in a time and place when things were different. According to Ray, back in Christopher, Illinois where he grew up in the 1930s, men were expected to respect women, work hard and come home dirty. He said women were expected to marry young, look *purdy*, and have supper ready at five every day. And kids like Ray, well they were expected to obey their parents, fear God, and love their country.

Ray once related to the daughter of an old friend, that until he had left southern Illinois he thought cars and pickup trucks were equipped with horns so as to allow their drivers to greet friends as they drove by. He didn't just grow up in a different time and place, he lived as though he *was* in a different time and place. And for those of us who knew him, we know it was a life unlike any other. Indeed, Ray had a *hanker'n* for life.

Christopher, Illinois circa 1956[10]

Every greeting, meeting, or event was for him, as he so affectionately liked to describe, *one hell of a barn-burner*. In fact, talking to strangers was one of Ray's favorite pastimes. Those who spent any quality time with him easily remember a time or two when Ray took up with a stranger and just started a conversation. He would never bring up the topics of politics, taxes, or current events. Instead, he'd ask them from where they came, about their upbringing, their first love, or their greatest loss. Ray wanted into their hearts. He expected nothing in return other than honesty.

More than once while quietly sitting outdoors he'd lean into me with a cupped hand to his mouth, as if to whisper a secret, and say, "See that guy (or gal) over there, wouldn't you just love to talk to them and find out who they are, where they grew up, and find out everything about them?"

Indeed, Dr. Ray Krug, DDS was the kind of friend you could sit next to on a porch swing, never say a word, and walk away feeling like it was the best conversation you've ever had. In his final days he and I had a lot of those kind of conversations. Among the many lessons he shared with me, the most insightful was that, "the happiest of people don't necessarily have the best of everything; they just make the most of the things that come their way." Friends are like that he said,—"make the most of every friend and friendship that comes your way."[11]

"We'll be friends forever, won't we, Pooh?" asked
Piglet. "Even longer," Pooh answered.
—*A. A. Milne,* Winnie-the-Pooh

The best way to destroy an enemy is to make
him a friend.
—*President, Abraham Lincoln*

Don't walk in front of me, I may not follow.
Don't walk behind me, I may not lead.

Just walk beside me and be my friend.
—*Albert Camus*

Do not save your loving speeches for your
friends 'til they are dead; do not write them on
their tombstones, speak them rather now instead.
—*Anna Commins*

A friend to all is a friend to none.
—*Aristotle*

The truth is, everyone is going to hurt you. You
just got to find the ones worth suffering for.
—*Bob Marley*

No man is a failure who has friends.
— *Clarence in a book inscription to George
from Frank Capra's* It's a Wonderful Life, *1946.*

True friendship is like sound health, the value of
it is seldom known until it be lost.
—*Charles Caleb Colton*

It is virtue, virtue, which both creates and
preserves friendship. On it depends harmony of
interest, permanence, fidelity.
—*Cicero*

False friends are like our shadow, keeping close
to us while we walk in the sunshine, but leaving
us the instant we cross into the shade.
—*Christian Nevell Bovee*

One measure of friendship consists not in the
number of things friends can discuss, but in the
number of things they need no longer mention.
—*Clifton Fadiman*

Friendship is unnecessary, like philosophy, like
art…It has no survival value; rather it is one of
those things which give value to survival.
—*C.S. Lewis*

There is nothing we like to see so much as the
gleam of pleasure in a person's eye when he feels
that we have sympathized with him, understood
him. At these moments, something fine and
spiritual passes between two friends. These are
the moments worth living.
—*Don Marquis*

Friendship with oneself is all-important, because
without it one cannot be friends with
anyone else in the world.
—*First Lady Eleanor Roosevelt*

A friend is someone who knows all about
you and still loves you.
—Elbert Hubbard

The real test of friendship is can you literally do
nothing with the other person? Can you enjoy
those moments of life that are utterly simple?
—Eugene Kennedy

It is not a lack of love, but a lack of friendship
that makes unhappy marriages.
—Friedrich Nietzsche

Be courteous to all, but intimate with few, and let
those few be well tried before you give
them your confidence.
—President, George Washington

Be true to your work, your word,
and your friends.
—Henry David Thoreau

There is nothing I would not do for those who
are really my friends. I have no notion of loving
people by halves, it is not my nature.
—Jane Austen

Some come and leave, fulfilling a single purpose;
others, for a time or a season to teach us by

sharing their experiences; and last, a select few
who participate forever with relationships
that endure through eternity.
—*Jaren L. Davis*

Treat all friends as you do your paintings
—place them in the best light.
—*Jennie Jerome Churchill*

Friends are the family you choose.
—*Jess C. Scott*

Being honest may not always get you a lot of
friends, but it'll always get you the right ones.
—*John Lennon*

I think if I've learned anything about friendship,
it's to hang in, stay connected, fight for them, and
let them fight for you. Don't walk away, don't be
distracted, don't be too busy or tired, don't take
them for granted. Friends are part of the glue that
holds life and faith together. Powerful stuff.
—*Jon Katz*

I always felt that the great high privilege, relief,
and comfort of friendship was that one
had to explain nothing.
—*Katherine Mansfield*

Friendship is always a sweet responsibility,
never an opportunity.
—*Khalil Gibran*

We all need friends with whom we can speak of
our deepest concerns, and who do not fear to
speak the truth in love to us.
—*Margaret Guenther*

It's the friends you can call up at
4 a.m. that matter.
—*Marlene Dietrich*

Friendship…is not something you learn in
school. But if you haven't learned the meaning of
friendship, you really haven't learned anything.
—*Muhammad Ali*

Sometimes being a friend means mastering the art
of timing. There is a time for silence. A time to
let go and allow people to hurl themselves into
their own destiny. And a time to prepare to pick
up the pieces when it's all over.
—*Octavia Butler*

Anybody can sympathize with the sufferings of a
friend, but it requires a very kind nature to
sympathize with a friends success.
—*Oscar Wilde*

There is a magnet in your heart that will attract
true friends. That magnet is unselfishness,
thinking of others first; when you learn to live for
others, they will live for you.
—*Paramahansa Yogananda*

The glory of friendship is not the outstretched
hand, not the kindly smile, nor the joy of
companionship; it is the spiritual inspiration that
comes to one when you discover that someone
else believes in you and is willing to
trust you with a friendship.
—*Ralph Waldo Emerson*

We cannot tell the precise moment when
friendship is formed. As in filling a vessel drop by
drop, there is at last a drop which makes it run
over; so in a series of kindnesses there is at last
one which makes the heart run over.
—*Ray Bradbury*

Don't be dismayed at goodbyes. A farewell is
necessary before you can meet again. And
meeting again, after moments or lifetimes is
certain for those who are friends.
—*Richard Bach*

The strongest marriage is between two who seek
the same God, the strongest friendship

between two who flee the same devil.
—*Robert Brault*

I value the friend who for me finds time on his
calendar, but I cherish the friend who for me
does not consult his calendar.
—*Robert Brault*

How does one keep from 'growing old inside'?
Surely only in community. The only way to make
friends with time is to stay friends with people…
Taking community seriously not only gives us the
companionship we need, it also relieves us of
the notion that we are indispensable.
—*Robert McAfee Brown*

Always set high value on spontaneous kindness.
He whose inclination prompts him to cultivate
your friendship of his own accord will love you
more than one whom you have been
at pains to attach to you.
—*Samuel Johnson*

But friendship is precious, not only in the shade,
but in the sunshine of life; and thanks to a
benevolent arrangement of things,
the greater part of life is sunshine.
—*President, Thomas Jefferson*

A true friend embosoms freely, advises justly,
assists readily, adventures boldly, takes all
patiently, defends courageously, and continues
a friend unchangeably.
—*William Penn*

A friend is one that knows you as you are,
understands where you have been, accepts
what you have become, and still,
gently allows you to grow.
—*William Shakespeare*

Anonymously…

A real friend never gets in your way unless you
happen to be going down.

If I had a flower for every time I thought of you
my friend…I could walk through this garden
called Life forever.

Friends are people with whom you dare to be
yourself. Your soul can be naked with them.

Friends encourage others to talk about
themselves. They say little about others and
rarely speak of their own success or pain. For
the truest friends are patient listeners.

You can make more friends in two months by
showing interest in others than you can in two
years by trying to get other people
interested in you.

Friendship isn't a big thing—
it's a million little things.

Friendship is like a bank account. You cannot
continue to draw upon it without
making periodic deposits.

Before you accept the opinion of a friend or
acquaintance who tells you that you are genius,
take a moment and reflect on what you thought
of their opinions in the past.

A good rule is not to talk about money with a
friend who has much more or
much less than you.

The reason dogs have so many friends is
because they wag their tails and
not their tongues.

Choose your friends by their character and your
socks by their color. Choosing your socks by
their character is vain, and choosing your friends
by their color is unthinkable.

A friend is someone who understands your past,
believes in your future, and accepts you
just the way you are.

True friends are those who care without
hesitation, remember without limitation, forgive
without any explanation, and love with
even little communication.

To each one of us friendship has a different
meaning. For all of us it is a gift. Friendship
needs to be cherished and nurtured. It needs to
be cultivated on a daily basis. Then shall it
germinate and yield its fruit.

Don't cry because it is over, smile
because it happened.

The words that escape a friend's mouth are 'I'll
be there when you say you need me,' but the
words that are unheard from a true friend's
heart are, 'I'll be there...whether you
say you need me or not.'

I came for friendship and left with love.

A friend of yours is a friend of mine.

And from the author…

A real friend is one who walks in at the very moment everyone else walks out.

It's funny they don't teach friendship in school, but it is in school we find our first friends.

Friendships can sometimes be painful, but let's face it, friends make life a lot more painless.

The best way to get a new friend is to be one.

Our best friends are happiest when we are, and suffer the most when we are not.

Never laugh at the dreams of a friend.

Before you remind a friend of his faults, reflect briefly on your own.

Envy is a waste of time and focus. But if you must, focus on the needs of others and waste time with a friend.

No friendship is tied with a bow, but every friendship is a gift.

All of us would like to have old friends. But old friends are not made in a hurry. If you would like to have such friends in the years to come, you had better start making new friends now. For our best friends are like good wine, they get better with time.

---

⁹ A quote similar to this has been attributed to Arnold H. Glasgow. See http://www.searchquotes.com/. However, the author has been unable to verify with any authority that Mr. Glasgow was indeed the first to have said it.

¹⁰ Photographer unknown. Source: http://www.wunderground.com/ Wximage/gjanello/0, obtained January 2014. Attempts to contact were unsuccessful.

¹¹ Ray and his wife, Claire, also loved dogs. For almost twenty-five years they rescued, raised, and trained dozens of Golden Labradors and graciously gifted them to those in need. Some recipients out lived their dogs and Ray and Claire had the pleasure of gifting them a second dog. According to Ray, many of the dogs provided more companionship to their recipients than the aid they were intended.

5 HOPE

Hope is the strength in your moment of weakness, the light in the dark, the fire when it's cold. Hope is more powerful than fear, and is the only antidote to despair. For when we have hope, we can face even the most difficult challenges in our path. Like courage, hope offers us the belief that failure is not fatal, but the strength to carry on when it is almost certain.

T rapped in a tiny dark cavern, Ariel sat, prayed, and contemplated all that was on the surface, nearly 3,000 feet above him. Buried alive with 32 other men on August 5, 2010 after the collapse of the main ramp at the copper and gold mine they worked, he waited. The mine was located in the Atacama Region of Chile; a place known for the quality of its minerals and as some believed, their spiritual powers. On the surface, for 17 days, family and friends waited for word that their loved ones were still alive. In this sweltering heat, deep underground, isolated from all that was above them, the men grew increasingly despondent. Unable to communicate with those on the surface, they prayed and consoled one another.

But unknown to them, family members, friends, journalists, and other strangers erected Camp Hope in the cool desert air above them and prayed as well. As tents were hoisted up and a statue of San Lorenzo, the patron saint of miners was carefully placed, people around the world clung to hope and faith. Ariel's wife, Elizabeth, pregnant with their third child, prayed with them for her husband's safe return.

Ariel, the father to two boys, 9 and 5, vowed to his wife only days before the collapse of the mine, that he would be present for their third child's birth. The day before the mining catastrophe, the couple had learned they would be having a little girl, and came to settle on the name Carolina. However, after his underground isolation, with meager rations of tuna and mackerel for days, it was in this darkness that Ariel first considered a different name for his daughter.

The first probe, or *paloma*, was sent down to the trapped miners on the 22nd of August to transport food, water, and other items necessary to their survival. Facing an uncertain future, Ariel shared a note with his wife with his request to rename their unborn daughter. Putting pen to paper, Ariel wrote, *"What if we call her Hope? Hope for the camp backing us, hope for getting us out of here, hope to keep fighting for my daughter, hope to unite my family."* Elizabeth agreed and after 40 days beneath the surface, with her husband's fate still uncertain, a small 7 pound bundle of hope was born. On September 14, 2010, Elizabeth gave birth to *Esperanza*, Spanish for hope.

When the news of Esperanza's birth reached the trapped miners, Hector, Ariel's father recalls, "Immediately it gave all the miners there a lot of excitement. They were all very happy about her birth and that she would be called Esperanza." There was a rare moment of cheer as the miners awaited their fate deep beneath the earth's surface.

On October 13, 2010, hope shone a light into the darkness, and the miners, 33 in all, were hoisted up one by one up through a narrow tube drilled by engineers above. It was a true feat of engineering genius and a triumph of faith and hope.

It was on October 13, the day he was rescued, that Ariel Ticona, surrounded by those with whom he was trapped for 69 days, held back tears as he held Esperanza for the first time. Ariel recalls, "[It was an] emotional moment," and simply described his new daughter as, "lovely." With an unknown future, Ariel and his fellow miners, clung to life, reached for the light, and had held out hope. Hope for their life. Hope for their family. Hope for those yet to be born.

The world watched that day, as the miners, who once worked below the ground for menial wages, were raised to a new life, full of promise and full of a once inconceivable hope.

Learn from yesterday, live for today, hope for
tomorrow. The important thing is not
to stop questioning.
—*Albert Einstein*

The grand essentials of happiness are: something
to do, something to love,

and something to hope for.
—*Allan Chalmers*

Hope begins in the dark, the stubborn hope that
if you just show up and try to do the right thing,
the dawn will come. You wait and watch and
work: you don't give up.
—*Anne Lammott*

The very least you can do in your life is to figure
out what you hope for. And the most you can do
is live inside that hope. Not admire it from a
distance but live right in it, under its roof.
—*Barbara Kingsolver*

The feeling of hopefulness sometimes comes
from someone helping us. Think back to a time
when you had lost hope. Many times we regained
our optimism because someone
gave us a helping hand.
—*Catherine Pulsifer*

Never let go of hope. One day you will see that it
all has finally come together. What you have
always wished for has finally come to be. You will
look back and laugh at what has passed
and you will ask yourself…
'How did I get through all of that?'
—*Charles L. Allen*

Of all the forces that make for a better world,
none is so indispensable, none so powerful, as
hope. Without hope men are only half alive. With
hope they dream and think and work.
—*Charles Sawyer*

Most of the important things in the world have
been accomplished by people who have kept on
trying when there seemed to be no hope at all.
—*Dale Carnegie*

Hope in a renewed future is one of the most
profound gifts of a life of faith.
—*David Hartman*

Hope is being able to see that there is light
despite all of the darkness.
—*Desmond Tutu*

All kids need is a little help, a little hope, and
somebody who believes in them.
—*Earvin Johnson*

Just as despair can come to one only from other
human beings, hope, too, can be given to one
only by other human beings.
—*Ellie Wiesel*

Where hope grows, miracles blossom.
—*Elna Rae*

What oxygen is to the lungs, such is hope
to the meaning of life.
—*Emil Brunner*

Hope is the thing with feathers, that perches in
the soul, and sings the tune without the words,
and never stops at all.
—*Emily Dickinson*

Hope is both the earliest and the most
indispensable virtue inherent in the state of being
alive. If life is to be sustained, hope must
remain, even where confidence is
wounded, trust impaired.
—*Erik H. Erikson*

Hope never abandons you, you abandon it.
—*George Weinberg*

To love means loving the unlovable. To forgive
means pardoning the unpardonable. Faith means
believing the unbelievable. Hope means hoping
when everything seems hopeless.
—*Gilbert Keith Chesterson*

To be hopeful in bad times is based on the fact
that human history is not only of cruelty, but also
of compassion, sacrifice, courage, kindness. If we
see only the worst, it destroys our capacity to do
something. If we remember those times and
places where people have behaved magnificently,
this gives us the energy to act. And if we do act,
in however small a way, we don't have to wait for
some grand Utopian future. The future is an
infinite succession of presents, and to live now as
we think human beings should live,
in defiance of all that is bad around us,
is itself a marvelous victory.
—*Howard Zinn*

In all things it is better to hope than to despair.
—*Johann Wolfgang von Goethe*

None of us can continue to grow, develop and
perform at our highest potential without hope.
Hope for success, hope for recognition, and
reward, and most importantly, hope supplies the
essential fuel that enables the human spirit to
continue moving forward, especially in
the face of severe adversity.
—*John Di Frances*

We should not let our fears hold us back
from pursuing our hopes.
—*President, John Fitzgerald Kennedy*

A prime function of a leader is
to keep hope alive.
—*John William Gardner*

Hope is a beautiful thing. It gives us peace and
strength, and keeps us going when all seems lost.
Accepting what you cannot change doesn't mean
you have given up on hope. It just means you
have to focus your hope on more humanly
tangible and attainable goals.
—*Julie Donner Anderson*

We postpone the finality of heartbreak by
clinging to hope. Though this might be
acceptable during early or transitional stages of
grief, ultimately it is no way to live. We need both
hands free to embrace life and accept love, and
that's impossible if one hand has a
death grip on the past.
—*Kristin Armstrong*

There is a crack in everything, that's
how the light gets in.
—*Leonard Cohen*

If you lose hope, somehow you lose the vitality
that keeps life moving, you lose the courage to
be, that quality that helps you go on in spite of it
all. And so today, I still have a dream.
—*Martin Luther King, Jr.*

God puts rainbows in the clouds so that each of
us—in the dreariest and most dreaded moments
—can see a possibility of hope.
—*Maya Angelou*

Hope is always available to us. When we feel
defeated, we need only take a deep breath and
say, "Yes," and hope will reappear.
—*Monroe Forester*

There is no medicine like hope, no incentive
so great, and no tonic so powerful as
expectation of something tomorrow.
—*Orison Swett Marden*

The value of another's experience is to give us
hope, not to tell us how or whether to proceed.
—*Peter Block*

Hope is the ability to hear the music of the
future; faith is the courage to dance to it today.
—*Peter Kuzmic*

Hope keeps you alive. Faith gives your life
meaning, blessings, and a good end.
—*Rex Rouis*

Hope is a powerful emotion that gives us
strength and helps us through trying and difficult

times. With hope, we believe that things will get
better, and we find the courage to keep trying.
—*Robert Alan Silverstein*

Where there is discord may we bring harmony.
Where there is error, may we bring truth.
Where there is doubt, may we bring faith.
Where there is despair, may we bring hope.
—*Saint Francis of Assisi*

The natural flights of the human mind are not
from pleasure to pleasure but from hope to hope.
—*Samuel Johnson*

Hope is the companion of power, and the mother
of success; for who so hopes strongly has
within him the gift of miracles.
—*Samuel Smiles*

Listen to the mustn'ts, child. Listen to the don'ts.
Listen to the shouldn'ts, the impossibles, the
won'ts. Listen to the never haves, then listen
close to me…Anything can happen, child.
Anything can be.
—*Shel Silverstein*

Hope is important because it can make the
present moment less difficult to bear. If we
believe that tomorrow will be better,

we can bear a hardship today.
—*Thich Nhat Hanh*

Man is, properly speaking, based upon hope, he
has no other possession but hope; this world of
his is emphatically the place of hope.
—*Thomas Carlyle*

Hope is not the conviction that something will
turn out well but the certainty that something
makes sense, regardless of how it turns out.
—*Vaclav Havel*

The word which God has written on the brow
of every man is Hope.
—*Victor Hugo*

Your hopes, dreams, and aspirations are
legitimate. They are trying to take you airborne,
above the clouds, above the storms,
if you only let them.
—*William James*

Anonymously…

When the world says, "Give up," hope whispers,
"Try one more time."

Never deprive someone of hope—
it may be all they have.

When the door of happiness closes, another
opens, but often times we look so long at the
closed door that we don't see the one which has
been opened for us.

When things are bad, we take comfort in the
thought that they could always be worse. And
when they are, we find hope in the thought that
things are so bad they have to get better.

He who has health, has hope. And he who has
hope, has everything.

And from the author…

Hope is a skill, without practice one
never seems to get good at it.

My hope is that courage trumps fear, my fear is
that those without hope are also without courage.

Those without hope are often helpless. Yet those
without help are never hopeless.

Were I granted a single wish, I hope I would
have the sense to make it a good one.

Hope is not a strategy, it's what's left for those
without a strategy.

Of all things, the sun is the most hopeful. It
never fails to rise, no matter how terrible
the day before.

*It takes courage to have hope. Courage is necessary because in spite of
all the hope we might muster, it seems, at times not enough. So isn't it
mysterious that acts of courage provide us hope while it is
hope that comforts the courageous?*

6 LOVE

---

*Love is an incredibly powerful word. We use it to describe an
unconditional affection which has no limits or expectations.
Love also leaves us with a sense of serenity and calm.
For when we are in love, our world seems
brighter, sharper, and more beautiful.
Love is—truly—a many-splendored thing.*

G race thought he was the most handsome man in the
world. Tall, strong, and determined, he was all any
young woman could have wanted. But all that
remained of him, was a small engagement ring which bound two
precious diamonds atop a small band of white gold.

Coming of age in Philadelphia in the late 40s was fun. It was a
bustling city filled with adventure, opportunity, and *men*. The War
had inspired great patriotism and many a teen, too young to serve,
searched for a way to serve their country—Grace was no
exception. As a teenager Grace dreamed of becoming a Navy
nurse. Unfortunately, a reaction to a vaccination she received
while in nursing school, ended her schooling and her dream.
Severely disappointed, she began to worry about her future.

But her stretch of bad luck would end on a warm June day in 1950. On a blind date, Grace, met the love of her life. Bob was a seagoing Marine, with an enormous heart and sparkling eyes. After their first date, Grace was smitten as a kitten, and indeed, bitten by love. The months that followed were bliss. Soon talk of matrimony arose. Grace's heart was on fire. Then Bob popped the big question and asked for her hand in marriage. Their engagement was sealed with a gorgeous diamond ring. But suddenly, much to her astonishment, Bob disappeared! Without explanation or even a simple good bye, he had vanished.

"The heck with him," Grace thought. At the time she was 21. Living with her parents and in a job she hated, the 5-foot-8-inch firebrand, decided to take matters into her own hands and join the Marines. After overcoming a small medical obstacle, she was accepted. Ten days later she left a note for her parents, saying only—"Joined the Marines. Gone to Paris Island." After her swearing-in at the Liberty Bell, with orders in hand, she boarded a train and headed to boot camp.

Unlike many of the other women in her platoon, Grace did not find the training difficult, nor the discipline intimidating. Raised by a German father (a policeman no less), and a Scottish mother, her "childhood was worse," she later admitted. The physical training, marching, and spit-shined boots and shoes also came easy. On graduation day, she and over 80 other women in her company were promoted to *private* in the United States Marine Corps. In celebration they sang, *The March of the Women Marines*. It goes, in part…"We serve so men may fight in air, on land, and sea. Marines! The eagle, globe, and anchor carry on to make men free *for me*." The "*for me*" was, of course, tacked on for a laugh. The young privates thought it was a gas.

Grace was like that, sharp witted, with an even sharper tongue. And in part because of it, she became a "plow-back." Such was the name given to those who stayed on at Paris Island as special instructors. These women were considered the best of the U.S. Marines. Not surprisingly, Grace knew it and showed it. Her performance was so impressive, Grace was later transferred to Washington D.C. to work for General Lemuel G. Shepherd, Jr., the Commandant of the Marine Corps.[12]

While there, Bob, the seagoing Marine who'd vanished several years before re-entered her life. She can no longer remember how they reunited, but the fire still burned in each of them. Several months later they were engaged again. The engagement did not last long. Several months after their engagement in October 1954, Bob called her one evening and broke it off. It wasn't another woman, he simply had cold feet. Heartbroken again, Grace trudged ahead in life without Bob.

In 1957 she left the Marine Corps and tried her hand at nursing school once more. And again she quit due to illness. "The work simply [made me sick]," she recalls. Then after a failed, twelve-year marriage, she re-entered school and this time graduated with degrees in sociology, psychology, and *nursing*. She eventually earned a master's degree and taught at Oklahoma Wesleyan University in Bartlesville.

Meanwhile, for 48 years Bob Meyers called another woman his wife. After her death in 2004, Bob once more thought of Grace and pondered the many years gone by. He was left with only a sad, "what-if?" But as luck would have it, while looking for a fellow Marine in an association directory, he found Grace. Fifty years and six weeks after he had broken off his second engagement with Grace, he called her the Sunday after Thanksgiving 2004.

The call lasted three and a half hours. They talked every night thereafter. During their call on New Year's Eve 2005, Bob proposed for a third time. Again Grace said yes! This time however, Grace Miltenberger-Meyers didn't need an engagement ring—she already had one. You see, Grace had kept the small diamond ring Bob first gave her more than 50 years prior. She had it taped to the bottom of a drawer for safe keeping, knowing one day she would need it. Bob and Grace married in November 2005 and have been happy ever since.

Love never dies a natural death. It dies because
we don't know how to replenish its source. It dies
of blindness and errors and betrayals. It dies of
illness and wounds; it dies of weariness, of
witherings, and of tarnishings.
—*Anais Nin*

Love is friendship that has caught fire. It is quiet
understanding, mutual confidence, sharing and
forgiving. It is loyalty through good and bad
times. It settles for less than perfection and
makes allowances for human weaknesses.
—*Ann Landers*

Life has taught us that love does not consist in
gazing at each other but in looking outward
together in the same direction.
—*Antoine de Saint-Exupéry*

In the end, only three things matter: how much
you loved, how gently you lived, and how
gracefully you let go of things
not meant for you.
—*Buddha*

True love is taking the risk that it won't be
happily-ever-after. True love is joining hands with
the man who loves you for who you are, and
saying, I'm not afraid to believe in you.
—*Cara Lockwood*

Once you truly believe you're worthy of love, you
will never settle for anyone's
second best treatment.
—*Charles J. Orlando*

Love is patient, love is kind. It does not envy, it
does not boast, it is not proud. It does not
dishonor others, it is not self-seeking, it is not
easily angered, it keeps no record of wrongs.
Love does not delight in evil but rejoices with the
truth. It always protects, always trusts,
always hopes, always preserves.
—*Corinthians 13:4-7*

To love at all is to be vulnerable. Love anything
and your heart will be wrung and possibly
broken. If you want to make sure of keeping it
intact you must give it to no one, not even an
animal. Wrap it carefully round with hobbies and
little luxuries; avoid all entanglements. Lock it up
safe in the casket or coffin of your selfishness.
But in that casket—safe, dark, motionless, airless,
it will change. It will not be broken; it will
become unbreakable, impenetrable, irredeemable.
To love is to be vulnerable.
—*C.S. Lewis*

Love doesn't need a reason. It speaks from the
irrational wisdom of the heart.
—*Deepak Chopra*

There are four questions of value in life… What
is sacred? Of what is the spirit made? What is
worth living for, and what is worth dying for?
The answer to each is the same. Only love.
—*Don Juan DeMarco*

You know you're in love when you can't fall
asleep because reality is finally better
than your dreams.
—*Dr. Seuss*

Love can defeat that nameless terror. Loving one
another, we take the sting from death.
—*Edward Abbey*

Love is the voice under all silences, the hope
which has no opposite in fear; the strength so
strong mere force is feebleness: the truth more
first than sun, more last than star.
—*E.E. Cummings*

A friend is someone who knows all about
you and still loves you.
—*Elbert Hubbard*

Immature love says, 'I love you because I need
you.' Mature love says, 'I need you
because I love you.'
—*Erich Fromm*

There are all kinds of love in this world
but never the same love twice.
—*F. Scott Fitzgerald*

There is only one happiness in life—
to love and to be loved.
—*George Sand*

The best and most beautiful things in this
world cannot be seen or even heard,

but must be felt with the heart.
—*Helen Keller*

Time is too slow for those who wait, too swift for
those who fear, too long for those who grieve,
too short for those who rejoice, but
for those who love, time is eternity.
—*Henry Van Dyke*

Love takes off masks that we fear we cannot live
without and know we cannot live within.
—*James Baldwin*

True love blossoms when we care more about
another person than we care about ourselves.
—*Elder Jeffrey R. Holland*

You don't love someone because they're perfect,
you love them in spite of the fact that they're not.
—*Jodi Picoult*

It is astonishing how little one feels
alone when one loves.
—*John Bulwer*

Love begins with a smile, grows with a
kiss, and ends with a tear.
—*Jordan Smith*

Love yourself first and everything else falls into line. You really have to love yourself to get anything done in this world.
—*Lucille Ball*

Darkness cannot drive out darkness: only light can do that. Hate cannot drive out hate: only love can do that.
—*Martin Luther King, Jr.*

Love one another and you will be happy. It's as simple and as difficult as that.
—*Michael Leunig*

The hunger for love is much more difficult to remove than the hunger for bread.
—*Mother Teresa*

Love comes more naturally to the human heart than its opposite.
—*Nelson Mandela*

Love is like the wind, you can't see it but you can feel it.
—*Nicholas Sparks*

If we deny love that is given to us, if we refuse to give love because we fear pain or loss, then our

lives will be empty, our loss greater.
—*Oprah Winfrey*

I love you without knowing how, or when, or
from where. I love you simply, without problems
or pride: I love you in this way because I do not
know any other way of loving but this, in which
there is no I or you, so intimate that when
I fall asleep your eyes close.
—*Pablo Neruda*

Love is that condition in which the happiness of
another person is essential to your own.
—*Robert A. Heinlein*

I would rather have eyes that cannot see; ears that
cannot hear; lips that cannot speak, than
a heart that cannot love.
—*Robert Tizon*

I love you, not because of who you are, but
because of who I am when I am with you.
—*Roy Croft*

What does love look like? It has the hands to help
others. It has the feet to hasten to the poor and
needy. It has the eyes to see misery and want. It
has the ears to hear the sighs and sorrows of
men. That is what love looks like.
—*Saint Augustine*

When you love someone…truly love them, friend
or lover, you lay your heart open to them. You
give them a part of yourself that you give to no
one else, and you let them inside a part of you
that only they can hurt—you literally hand them
the razor with a map of where to cut deepest
and most painfully on your heart and soul.
—*Sherrilyn Kenyon*

We accept the love we think we deserve.
—*Stephen Chbosky*

I learned the real meaning of love. Love is
absolute loyalty. People fade, but loyalty never
fades. You can depend so much on certain
people, you can set your watch by them. And
that's love, even if it doesn't seem very exciting.
—*Sylvester Stallone*

The most precious gift we can offer anyone is our
attention. When mindfulness embraces those
we love, they will bloom like flowers.
—*Thich Nhat Hanh*

The greatest happiness of life is the conviction
that we are loved; loved for ourselves, or rather,
loved in spite of ourselves.
—*Victor Hugo*

Love is the ability and willingness to allow those
that you care for to be what they choose for
themselves, without any insistence
that they satisfy you.
—*Wayne Dyer*

Anonymously...

I don't pretend to know what love is for
everyone, but I can tell you what love is for me;
love is knowing all about someone, and still
wanting to be with them more than any other
person, love is trusting them enough to tell them
everything about yourself, including the things
you might be ashamed of, love is feeling
comfortable and safe with someone, but still
getting weak knees when they walk
into a room and smile at you.

It takes only a minute to get a crush on someone,
an hour to like someone, and a day to love
someone—but a lifetime to forget someone.

The best love is the one that makes you a better
person, without changing you into
someone other than yourself.

Maybe God wants us to meet a few wrong people
before meeting the right one so that when we

finally meet the right person, we will know how
to be grateful for that gift.

The strongest actions for a woman are to love
herself, be herself, and shine amongst those who
never believed she could.

It's true that we don't know what we've got until
we lose it, but it's also true that we don't know
what we've been missing until it arrives.

To the world you may be one person,
but to one person you may be the world.

Just because someone doesn't love you the way
you want them to doesn't mean they don't love
you with all they have.

And from the author…

Never frown, even when sad, because you never
know who is watching you and falling in
love with your smile.

Love often comes when we least expect it,
but seems to leave when we come to expect it.

Love mends hate
and hate squanders love.

You don't find love, it finds you—often, where
and when we least expect it.

*Mark Twain once said "I could live for two months on a good
compliment." Words of Affirmation are the priceless verbal expressions of
true love. Simple statements of appreciation and compliments offer
encouragement and express gratitude. Such words communicate we are
paying attention and that which our partner does and says are important.
Words of Affirmation transcend the simple words,
"I love you," by validating them.*[13]

---

[12] General Shepherd was the first Commandant to serve on the Joint Chiefs
of Staff.

[13] Dr. Gary D. Chapman coined the term, "Words of Affirmation." His
book, *The Five Love Languages: The Secret to Love that Lasts*, is a consistent *New
York Times* bestseller and has sold over 5 million copies.

7 FAMILY

---

*Family is one of man's oldest and grandest institutions. It
enables its members to be part of something greater than
themselves or merely part of a group. Within our family we
most often have people that share our values and morals. It
isn't about blood or lineage, but rather about unconditional
love and acceptance. Our family enables us to forget
ourselves and elevate the importance of others.*[14]

I t started like any other ordinary spring day. Bright sunshine
and warm air filled with the giggles and squeals of playing
children. However, this particular day in gym class was
going to be different. The teacher in charge of the fifth graders
began the period by handing out tickets to a local skating rink.
She told the eager recipients they were rewards for positive
behavior and good sportsmanship. At dismissal, however, Jaci
was approached by one of her students stating he wished to speak
to her. With considerable shyness, one of the young students
solemnly explained that the ticket he was given for skating would
be wasted on him.

You see, until this day, Jaci wasn't aware of the struggle this 10-

year-old boy hid from his classmates and teachers. This young student was in foster care, and lived in a group home. After his mother was jailed on drug charges and his father abandoned him; he simply had nowhere else to go, and no one that would take him. "My heart just broke," Jaci recalls, as she remembers this young boy's circumstances.

That day served as the catalyst for the events that would soon follow. Little did Jaci know, this one child prompted what would become her family's legacy. Soon, Jaci and her husband, Eric, began researching, and quickly learned that this situation was not just one young little boy's fate, but the predicament of so many other girls and boys in their area. It was then that they sat down with their three biological children, 6, 7, and 8 at the time, and agreed that they would embark on a journey that would redefine all prior notions of what made up their family. Two years after handing out coupons to a local skating rink, on what she now realizes was anything but an ordinary day in 1996, the first children arrived, two sisters, 4 and 9, and their 18-month old half-brother. Jaci and Eric became foster parents.

Since that day, more than 30 children, mostly abused or neglected, have come to live in their home. "The kids came with a lot of anger, fear, and trust issues," Jaci said. One of the youngest children, Levi, was born in a car to his two homeless parents. With severe facial deformities, Levi came to learn from his new family what unconditional love truly meant. In all, Jaci and Eric have personally adopted nine of their foster children, whose fate might otherwise have been bleak. "Some kids stick around for three days until a relative can be found to take care of them, some for three weeks, some for six months to a year until the parents get things together, and for the rest of the kids—a lifetime," Jaci says. "Our philosophy has always been that if a child is not returned to [his or] her parents or relatives or moved elsewhere by the court, then our home would be their final stop, their 'forever home'."

In 2001, Jaci and Eric's magnanimous ideal of family grew to inspire four other couples, in the Riverside, California community. As the foster and adoptive families in their community grew, Eric and Jaci began to notice another opportunity to support their area and the children they cared so much about. Seeing the need, once again, Jaci and Eric were inspired to formalize their role by starting a support group for foster and adoptive parents. Eric quit his high-paying job as a stockbroker and went back to school to get his master's degree in counseling.

After obtaining his degree, Eric began counseling those looking to foster or adopt, as well as mothers who were considering giving up their children. Soon after, the couple's eldest daughter Krista, founded the Walk Your Talk Walk, to raise awareness for the needs of foster children, like those she now considers her younger brothers and sisters.[15]

Although Jaci and Eric Hasemeyer are not planning to expand their family further, they hope their story of love, acceptance, generosity, and compassion will encourage others to become foster and adoptive parents, and reconsider how they previously defined family. These virtuous individuals embody what it means to be a family, and understand, that a family is not born from DNA, but is bonded together out of love.

I know why families were created with all their
imperfections. They humanize you. They are
made to make you forget yourself occasionally, so
that the beautiful balance of life is not destroyed.
—*Anais Nin*

Without a family, man, alone in the world,
trembles in the cold.
—*Andre Maurois*

Other things may change us, but we
start and end with family.
—*Anthony Brandt*

Everyone needs a house to live in, but a
supportive family is what builds a home.
—*Anthony Liccione*

Special people in our life sometimes can become
our family, it doesn't mean they
have to be blood related.
—*B.B. Butler*

Some of the most important conversations I've
ever had occurred at my family's dinner table.
—*Bob Ehrlich*

Families are the compass that guide us. They are
the inspiration to reach great heights, and our

comfort when we occasionally falter.
—*Brad Henry*

There is no such thing as a perfect family. Behind every door there are issues, the difference is accepting each family member as they are, not as we would like them to be.
—*Catherine Pulsifer*

The family is the most basic unit of government. As the first community to which a person is attached and the first authority under which a person learns to live, the family established society's most basic values.
—*Charles Caleb Colton*

The love of family and the admiration of friends is much more important than wealth and privilege.
—*Charles Kuralt*

To put the world right in order, we must first put the nation in order; to put the nation in order, we must first put the family in order; to put the family in order, we must first cultivate our personal life; we must first set our hearts right.
—*Confucius*

Family means no one gets left behind
or forgotten.
—*David Ogden Stiers*

That's what people do who love you. They put
their arms around you and love you
when you're not so lovable.
—*Deb Caletti*

You don't choose your family. They are God's
gift to you, as you are to them.
—*Desmond Tutu*

When we think of our family, our spouse,
parents, or children, let us see them
as a gift from God.
—*Dillon Burroughs*

The family – that dear octopus from whose
tentacles we never quite escape, nor, in our
inmost hearts, ever quite wish to.
—*Dodie Smith*

You are born into your family and your family is
born into you. No returns. No exchanges.
—*Elizabeth Berg*

You can kiss your family and friends good-bye
and put miles between you, but at the same time

you carry them with you in your heart,
your mind, your stomach, because you do
not just live in a world but a world lives in you.
—*Frederick Buechner*

Family faces are magic mirrors looking at people
who belong to us, we see the past,
present, and future.
—*Gail Lumet Buckley*

What greater thing is there for human souls than
to feel that they were joined for life – to be with
each other in silent unspeakable memories.
—*George Eliot*

The family is the test of freedom; because the
family is the only thing that the free man makes
for himself and by himself.
—*Gilbert K. Chesterton*

The children have been a wonderful gift to me,
and I'm thankful to have once again seen our
world through their eyes. They restore my faith
in the family's future.
—*First Lady Jacqueline Lee Kennedy,*

Call it a clan, call it a network, call it a tribe,
call it a family: Whatever you call it,
whoever you are, you need one.
—*Jane Howard*

There's nothing that makes you more insane than
family. Or more happy. Or more exasperated.
Or more secure.
—*Jim Butcher*

The great gift of family life is to be intimately
acquainted with people you might never even
introduce yourself to, had life not done it for you.
—*Kendall Hailey*

Family is essential because we all yearn to belong
to something greater than ourselves.
—*Laura Ramirez*

No matter what you've done for yourself or for
humanity, if you can't look back on having
given love and attention to your own family,
what have you really accomplished?
—*Lee Iacocca*

The family is the cornerstone of our society.
More than any other force it shapes the attitude,
the hopes, the ambitions, and the values of the
child. And when the family collapses it is the
children that are usually damaged. When it
happens on a massive scale the community itself
is crippled. So, unless we work to strengthen the
family, to create conditions under which most
parents will stay together, all the rest—schools,
playgrounds, and public assistance,
and private concern—will never be enough.
—*President, Lyndon Baines Johnson*

The best inheritance a parent can give to his
children is a few minutes of their time each day.
—*M. Grundler*

The strength of a family, like the strength of an
army, is in its loyalty to each other.
—*Mario Puzo*

Sometimes the best families are the ones God
builds using unexpected pieces of our hearts.
—*Melanie Shankle*

Family is not an important thing.
It's everything.
—*Michael J. Fox*

Let us make one point, that we meet each other
with a smile, when it is difficult to smile. Smile at
each other, make time for each
other in your family.
—*Mother Theresa*

A family is a unit composed not only of children
but of men, women, an occasional animal,
and the common cold.
—*Ogden Nash*

Our most basic instinct is not for survival but for
family. Most of us would give our own life for the

survival of a family member, yet we lead our
daily life too often as if we take our
family for granted.
—*Paul Pearshall*

It didn't matter how big our house was; it
mattered that there was love in it.
—*Peter Buffett*

The great danger for family life, in the midst of
any society whose idols are pleasure, comfort,
and independence, lies in the fact that people
close their hearts and become selfish.
—*Pope John Paul II*

The bond that links your true family is not one of
blood, but of respect and joy in each other's life.
Rarely do members of one family
grow up under the same roof.
—*Richard Bach*

The best part of life is when your family become
your friends and your friends
become your family.
—*Robin Roberts*

I cannot think of any need in childhood as strong
as the need for a father's protection.
—*Sigmund Freud*

Family life is full of major and minor crises—the ups and downs of health, success and failure in career, marriage, and divorce—and all kinds of characters. It is tied to places and events and histories. With all of these felt details, life etches itself into memory and personality. It's difficult to imagine anything more nourishing to the soul.
—*Thomas Moore*

A man should never neglect his family for business [or another woman].
—*Walt Disney*

There is no doubt that it is around the family and the home that all the greatest virtues, the most dominating virtues of human society, are created, strengthened, and maintained.
—*Sir Winston Churchill*

Anonymously...

Families are like fudge—mostly sweet but more interesting with a few nuts.

If you have a family that loves you, a few good friends, food on your table, and a roof over your head, you are richer than you think.

The most important things in life are your
friends, family, health, good humor, and a
positive attitude towards life. If you have these
then you have everything!

And from the author…

Children learn to smile, hate, fear, enjoy life, love,
laugh and cry from their parents.

Raising a family is risky business, the greater the
love, the greater the potential loss.

Children are the symbol of the eternal marriage
of love and duty.

Insanity doesn't run in my family, it gallops.

A mother's love is unconditional. It need not be
acquired, nor it deserved. However, it is perishable
and if not nurtured it will
easily wilt and spoil.

If having a happy family were easy, everybody
would have one.

Dinner at five every night was the rule in my
family—so were chores, completing your
homework, respecting your elders, saying please
and thank you, and most of all,
holding an unshakable faith in God.

If I had a dime every time my father had to remind
me to take out the trash after dinner I'd be a
millionaire. If he were here to remind me one more
time, I'd be a millionaire a million times over.

*Recently while attending the funeral of a beloved uncle,
a peacefulness came over me as I heard someone say,
"He lived his whole life, for this moment." It was then that it hit me—
his was a life that spoke to us. His gift was the ability to speak the truth
when inconvenient, stand tall in the face of opposition, respond with
kindness when treated harshly, and laugh in the face of uncertainty. Eddie
Sheehan was a Long Island bayman of the finest kind. His gift was
intended for his family but as I witnessed at his service, he shared it with all
those who knew him. In doing so, he made family of all of us.*

---

14 *Family* is generally not considered a virtue. However, the author thought
it of such importance to the development and the cultivation of virtuosity
among those in the family unit, he chose to include it.
15 To learn more about the Walk Your Talk Walk, or to learn more about
how you can help this worthy cause visit http://walkyourtalkwalk.info/

8 Wisdom

Wisdom is the ability to think and act using one's knowledge, experience, insight, and common sense. It is not inherited nor is it easily taught. It is innate and is expressed as a disposition to think and behave with a willingness to consistently apply perception and judgment with passion and reason. As such, it is the rarest of all virtues—and arguably, the most valuable.

I t was a hot, sticky, end-of-summer day. The air was heavy and not a blade of grass moved in its stillness. It mattered little to Jean, school was out, and it was summer in Missouri, a time to play, explore, and dream. It was also a time when children had chores and on the small farm in which she lived, there were many. Of them, least enjoyed was collecting the mail. About a mile's distance by road, the shortest path was through fields and thickets, across creeks, and a shallow river.

"Take the bucket with you," her grandmother instructed. Handing Jean the very familiar half-gallon syrup bucket. "What for?" she replied. The season was nearly over, spring's offerings had either been picked or gone to seed she thought. "You'll find something to fill it," her grandmother replied with a gentle smile. The little nine-year-old begrudgingly complied; singing and swinging the bucket as she skipped away.

She had carried a bucket a good portion of her life. Twice a day she lugged pails of milk, then used a pail to feed the chickens, bring salt to the cows, and carry molasses to her neighbors. Some days it seemed as if a bucket was her only friend.

Halfway to the mailbox, she stopped and rested. Under the shade of a large oak, looking down at the steel pail in her hand, she decided "I needn't carry it the whole way," and left it near a pokeberry bush.

Arriving soon at the cluster of dusty old mailboxes aside the road, finding no mail and no one to talk to, she turned about and went back for the bucket. Upon finding it, she discovered a few ripe pokeberries had fallen into it. She proceeded to pick off enough clusters of the dark bitter berries to fill the pail, even though she thought they were "good for nothing."

"Aren't they just lovely?" Grandma exclaimed admiringly as Jean set them on the kitchen table. *But what to do with them?* was the look on the woman's face. "Ah, we'll make some pokeberry ink!" she exclaimed. With that, she filled a small cloth tobacco sack with the berries and squeezed out their juice. When finished, grandmother and granddaughter sat and used the vibrant magenta ink and penned a few overdue letters to distant cousins.

The next day, Jean again carried the bucket; this time taking it a little farther than the previous day before eventually setting it down. But again no mail. Returning to the bucket, she found it empty. "Sad," she thought to herself, "a little empty pail." About to go, she looked up and caught sight of a clump of peppermint growing close to the path. She had passed it every day and never noticed it before. "Peppermint doesn't just spring up overnight," she thought to herself. So she picked a bucketful and noticed its pungent aroma seemed to cool the hot day.

Grandma was delighted with the peppermint. She liked to chew it, make tea with it, use it in stews and hold it to her nose. "My, the freshness almost leaves one breathless."

And so it went, as the summer wore on, the daily admonition to carry the bucket was repeated day-in and day-out. Jean, years later recalled, "Slowly, then more quickly I began to see other things. Things I had never seen before." Jean remembers the jewelweed bloom along the riverbank, an abandoned oriole's nest dangling from the high elm limb, and wondrous, yes wondrous, majestic clouds. Even a patch of common sumac seemed remarkable. Brilliantly red, shaped like a big, open umbrella waiting for a fresh autumn rain she thought. When she described it to her grandmother, he grandmother looked at her and slowly smiled. "Somehow I knew I'd pleased her, for what, I did not know," Jean reflected.

Then, several days later for the first time, Jean noticed the most captivating sight yet, a butterfly migration. Dozens and dozens of monarchs drifted above her, bright orange and black, as if they had all the time in the world. She imagined she was one of them; light, beautiful, and free like the breeze. Daydreaming the entire way, she returned to the tiny farmhouse. Her bucket was empty, "I forgot all about filling it when I saw the butterflies," she apologized to her waiting grandmother. In every magnificent detail, Jean told her what she had experienced. Grandma sat and listened intently, with a broad, knowing smile that only a wise grandmother could render.

The next day, when she picked up the bucket before leaving for the mailbox, Grandma's hand closed over hers and gently loosened little Jean Bell Mosley's hold. "Honey," she said, "you don't need the bucket anymore."

Jean Bell Mosley's was born September 21, 1913, in St. Francois County, Missouri. It was a magical place in a magical time. A simpler time. A time of peace, humble prosperity, and great American expectations. It was a place of diverse wildlife, wide meadows, small farms, and gentle, winding streams. And it was in this place, her home on a simple farm, she learned through the wisdom of her grandmother, appreciation for the beauty and wonder of nature—*and life.*

Little Jean Bell Mosley would one day become a widely-read and popular author. Using the wisdom of her grandmother, she learned to paint with words.[16] And for that, we are grateful.[17]

Memory is the mother of all wisdom.
—*Aeschylus*

Wisdom is not a product of schooling but of the
lifelong attempt to acquire it.
—*Albert Einstein*

All human wisdom is summed up in two words—
wait and hope.
—*Alexandre Dumas*

Knowing yourself is the beginning of all wisdom.
—*Aristotle*

The doorstep to the temple of wisdom is a
knowledge of our own ignorance.
—*Benjamin Franklin*

The whole problem with the world is that fools
and fanatics are always so certain of themselves,
and wiser people so full of doubts.
—*Bertrand Russell*

The wise man lets go of all results, whether good
or bad, and is focused on the action alone.
—*Bhagavad Gita*

Wisdom is more precious than rubies.
—*Bible, Proverbs 3:15*

A wise man can learn more from a foolish
question than a fool can learn from a wise answer.
—*Bruce Lee*

Wisdom is the right use of knowledge. To know is not to be wise. Many men know a great deal, and are all the greater fools for it. There is no fool so great a fool as a knowing fool. But to know how to use knowledge is to have wisdom.
—*Charles Spurgeon*

A single conversation across the table with a wise man is worth a month's study of books.
—*Chinese Proverb*

By three methods we may learn wisdom: first by reflection, which is noblest; second, by imitation, which is easiest; and third by experience, which is the bitterest.
—*Confucius*

A wise man proportions his beliefs to the evidence.
—*David Hume*

Wisdom is knowing what to do next, skill is knowing how to do it, and virtue is doing it.
—*David Starr Jordan*

Wisdom is the reward you get for a lifetime of listening when you'd have preferred to talk.
—*Doug Larson*

To everything there is a season, and a time
to every purpose under the heaven.
—*Ecclesiastes 3:1*

Wisdom comes with the ability to be still. Just look
and just listen. No more is needed. Being still,
looking, and listening activates the non-conceptual
intelligence within you. Let stillness
direct your words and actions.
—*Eckhart Tolle*

One must spend time in gathering knowledge
to give it out richly.
—*Edward C. Steadman*

Mothers, teach your children this. Teach your
children that wisdom is everywhere. In pieces.
Some of the wisdom is in the trees, some of the
wisdom is with the animals. Some of the wisdom is
with the planets and the stars and the moons and
the sun. Some of the wisdom was with our
ancestors. Some of the wisdom is in our minds. All
of the wisdom is from the Spirit of God.
—*Esther Davis-Thomas*

We are made wise not by the recollection of our
past, but by the responsibility for our future.
—*George Bernard Shaw*

The wise person questions himself,
the fool questions others.
—*Henri Arnold*

Many men go fishing all of their lives without
knowing that it is not fish they are after.
—*Henry David Thoreau*

Wisdom is not communicable. The wisdom which
a wise man tries to communicate always sounds
foolish… Knowledge can be communicated, but
not wisdom. One can find it, live it, do
wonders through it, but one cannot
communicate and teach it.
—*Hermann Hesse*

Wisdom is not wisdom when it is
derived from books alone.
—*Horace*

Wisdom is the power to see and the inclination to
choose the best and highest goal, together with the
surest means of attaining it.
—*J.I. Packer*

Knowledge speaks, but wisdom listens.
—*Jimi Hendrix*

We seem to gain wisdom more readily through our
failures than through our successes. We always
think of failure as the antithesis of success, but it
isn't. Success often lies just the
other side of failure.
—*Leo Buscaglia*

In seeking wisdom thou art wise; in imagining that
thou hast attained it—thou art a fool.
—*Lord Chesterfield*

It is unwise to be too sure of one's own wisdom. It
is healthy to be reminded that the strongest might
weaken and the wisest might err.
—*Mahatma Gandhi*

There is no man...however wise, who has not at
some period of his youth said things, or lived a life,
the memory of which is so unpleasant to him that
he would gladly expunge it. And yet he ought not
entirely regret it, because he cannot be certain that
he has indeed become a wise man—so far as it is
possible for any of us to be wise—unless he has
passed through all the fatuous or unwholesome
incarnations by which that ultimate
stage must be preceded.
—*Marcel Proust*

To acquire knowledge, one must study, but to
acquire wisdom, one must observe.
—*Marilyn vos Savant*

A wise woman wishes to be no one's enemy; a
wise woman refuses to be anyone's victim.
—*Maya Angelou*

The young man knows the rules, but the old
man knows the exceptions.
—*Oliver Wendell Holmes, Sr.*

Wisdom is like electricity. There is no permanently
wise man, but men capable of wisdom, who, being
put into certain company, or other favorable
conditions, become wise for a short time, as
glasses rubbed acquire electric power for a while.
—*Ralph Waldo Emerson*

Patience is the companion of wisdom.
—*Saint Augustine*

Though wisdom cannot be gotten with gold,
still less can be gotten without it.
—*Samuel Butler*

Common sense in an uncommon degree is what
the world calls wisdom.
—*Samuel Taylor Coleridge*

Never mistake knowledge for wisdom. One helps
you make a living; the other helps you make a life.
—*Sandra Carey*

Wisdom does not show itself so much in precept
as in life – in firmness of mind and a mastery of
appetite. It teaches us to do as well as to talk; and
to make our words and actions all of a color.
—*Seneca*

True wisdom comes to each of us when we realize
how little we understand about life, ourselves,
and the world around us.
—*Socrates*

The first step in the acquisition of wisdom is
silence, the second listening, the third memory, the
fourth practice, the fifth teaching others.
—*Solomon Ibn Gabriol*

Wisdom outweighs any wealth.
—*Sophocles*

God grant me the serenity to accept the things I
cannot change, courage to change the things I can,
and the wisdom to know the difference.
—*The Serenity Prayer*

Great is wisdom; infinite is the value of wisdom. It

cannot be exaggerated; it is the highest
achievement of man.
—*Thomas Carlyle*

The wise know too well their weakness to assume
infallibility; and he who knows must know
best how little he knows.
—*President, Thomas Jefferson*

The writings of the wise are the only riches our
posterity cannot squander.
—*Walter Savage Landor*

Knowledge is proud that she knows so much;
Wisdom is humble that she knows no more.
—*William Cowper*

The art of being wise is the art of
knowing what to overlook.
—*William James*

Good people are good because they've come
to wisdom through failure.
—*William Saroyan*

Wisdom doesn't necessarily come with age.
Sometimes age just shows up all by itself.
—*President, Woodrow T. Wilson*

Anonymously...

The wisest man is he who does not
believe he is wise.

Knowing others is intelligence; knowing yourself is
true wisdom. Mastering others is strength;
mastering yourself is true power.

The way of a great man is three fold; virtuous,
he is free from anxieties; wise, he is free from
perplexities; and bold he is free from fear.[18]

And from the author...

It seems for some, what they lack in wisdom,
they offer in advice.

Not a tenth part of my wisdom is my own.

It is through old things we learn
that which is new.

Fear less, hope more, whine less, do more,
talk less, pray more, and good things will be yours.

Wisdom can either be earned or purchased. Those
who choose to purchase it, often find it is
easier earned.

Conventional wisdom is a myth. For if it existed,
wisdom would not be in such short supply.

If results are a testament to our wisdom,
I wish I were wiser.

After his resignation from the Supreme Court, at the age of ninety-one,
Oliver Wendell Holmes, Jr. spent the summer at his country
house in Massachusetts. Several old friends from Boston came to visit,
bringing along their grandchildren, whose company he immensely enjoyed.
Sitting on the porch one day, Holmes fell into conversation with
Betsy Warder, then sixteen. "I won't refrain from talking
about anything because you're too young," he remarked
with a smile, "if you won't because I'm too old."

---

[16] Later as an adult, she became a teacher and taught school for a short time. She then became an executive secretary and accountant and managed an insurance agency during World War II while its owner served our country overseas. She wrote at night and sold her first story to *Woman's Day* magazine. Her first book, *The Mockingbird Piano*, was published in 1953, and won the Missouri Writers' Guild Award. Her subsequent books were successes as well, as were her short stories and articles that appeared in *Reader's Digest, Saturday Evening Post, Ladies Home Journal, Farm Journal, Country Gentleman*, and many other publications.

[17] Adapted from a story authored by Ms. Mosley entitled, *The Summer I learned to Really See* as published in *Readers Digest Magazine* in 1977.

[18] An axiom similar to this one has been credited to Confucius. However, because of the many versions found, the author chose to cite it as *anonymous* and apologizes to Confucius.

9 HONESTY

Honesty is more than not lying. It is being sincere and kind, thoughtful and thought-provoking. Honest people don't hide their deeds and often share their failures, for they know that to believe in something and not to share it, is dishonest.

W hat if you were poor, living a lie, and living in the shadows? What if you were a foreigner in a foreign land, far from home and all that was familiar? What if you lived in a country of abundance and plenty and yet you had nothing? Ascension was such a person, afraid, alone, and unable to speak the language of those around him.

He had come from the poor Mexican farming town, Tepeapulco, Hidalgo. It was an ancient place, once under the rule of the Aztec Empire, and it was as beautiful as it was humble. With opportunity and luck scarce, his parents couldn't afford to educate him beyond grade school. So like his father, he worked as a laborer-carpenter. His mother cleaned homes and toiled at menial tasks to help make ends meet. Ascension promised her he would one day help and bring fortune to his unfortunate family.

So out of desperation and scarcity, Ascension left home and journeyed to the City of Angels.

There in Los Angeles, California he found work. For 10 hours a day, six days a week, he labored in the scullery of a rundown Chinese restaurant for a mere $1300 a month. Then one day his luck changed. Alone, while waiting at a bus stop, an armored truck rumbled by. To his amazement, as it passed making a sharp turn around the corner on which he stood, its rear doors swung open and out dropped a large canvas bag. As the truck sped away, in front of him laid a solitary, unopened bag. Looking quickly in both directions as if to see if he was being watched, he cautiously approached the bag, grabbed it, and took it to the curb. Peeking inside he found what was to be $203,000 in cash.

Should he keep it or find its owner and return it? What if he kept it—would anyone ever know? What if he attempted to return it and the authorities thought that he had stolen it? Ascension, a 22-year-old undocumented restaurant dishwasher knew at once he was facing what might be a life-changing dilemma. His mind churned as he attempted to sort his options. Panicked, he hailed a passing cab and returned home. There in a run-down inner city apartment he shared with five other men, he sat looking down on the bulging canvas bag.

Like Ascension, his five companions soon returned from work. With them he shared his story, and together they discussed what to do with the money. Several thought it was a gift from God and that he should graciously accept it. Two thought he should return it or maybe just throw it away. Confused, Ascension decided to sleep on it and make a decision the next morning. But sleep didn't come easy, all night he tossed and turned. His mind would not quiet. He had lived frugally and often sent as much as $600 home each month. Then suddenly destiny had given him a staggering sum of money. So much he thought, he could finally build his mother her cinder block dream home, provide financial security for his family and live the life he had always aspired. He could return to Tepeapulco, a city of 45,000 people and be a hero.

However, the next morning when Ascension awoke he turned on the television and all over the news was the story of the missing $203,000. The armored transport company that had lost the money was offering a $25,000 reward for its return. But what shook him was a question raised by one of the reporters—*was there anyone honest enough to return the money?* At once, Ascension knew what he had to do. Without hesitation and without further thought, he called the police. Fearful of immigration authorities seizing and deporting him, he agreed to meet the police at a nearby baseball field. Arriving minutes later, he handed over the bag filled with the money he had found.

"I find it really hard to believe in this day and age that we have someone honest enough to turn in $203,000," police Sgt. Rick Sanchez told the *Los Angeles Times*. "He upholds the highest honor of [citizenship]." And so the accolades came. Ascension became the hero he had dreamed. And yes he received his $25,000 reward. But with it came more media and more publicity. Soon his story was shared all over the world.

When the story was broadcast on television in Tepeapulco, his mother told the *Times* reporter, "I cried of joy." And with humor, she added, "He seemed a little gordito," (chubby), in reference to him appearing heavier on TV than he was when she last saw him two years earlier. "I thought it was a miracle from God—that God illuminated the path for him. We're very proud of our son. Honesty is something we inculcated in him." His father was proud of him as well. "[M]any also congratulate us for having such a son. They speak to us with respect."

Ascension Franco Gonzales paid $8,000 in federal and state taxes and check cashing fees upon receipt of his reward that August in 2001. With that which remained he financed the construction of his mother's dream home in which she lives to this day. And to the amazement of everyone, U.S. Immigration and Naturalization Service took no action against Ascension. He later returned to the sleepy town of Tepeapulco.

Anyone who doesn't take truth seriously in small
matters cannot be trusted in large ones either.
—*Albert Einstein*

The most exhausting thing in life
is being insincere.
—*Anne Lindbergh*

Liars when they tell the truth are not believed.
—*Aristotle*

The best measure of a man's honesty isn't his
income tax return. It's the zero adjust
on his bathroom scale.
—*Arthur C. Clarke*

Living with integrity means: Not settling for less
than what you know you deserve in relationships.
Asking for what you want and need from others.
Speaking your truth, even though it might
create conflict or tension. Behaving in ways that
are in harmony with your personal values.
Making choices based on what you believe,
and not what others believe.
—*Barbara De Angelis*

Honest hearts produce honest actions.
—*Brigham Young*

Honesty has a beautiful and refreshing simplicity
about it. No ulterior motives. No hidden
meanings. An absence of hypocrisy, duplicity,
political games, and verbal superficiality. As
honesty and real integrity characterize our lives,
there will be no need to manipulate others.
—*Charles Swindoll*

Slander cannot destroy the honest man – when the
flood recedes the rock is there.
—*Chinese Proverb*

The first step toward greatness is to be honest,
says the proverb; but the proverb fails to state the
case strong enough. Honesty is not only "the first
step toward greatness,"—it is greatness itself.
—*Christian Nestell Bovee*

Honest actions build a good reputation.
—*Donna B. Forrest*

Honesty is the single most important factor having
a direct bearing on the final success of an
individual, corporation, or product.
—*Ed McMahon*

People grow through experience if they
meet life honestly and courageously.
This is how character is built.
—*First Lady Eleanor Roosevelt*

Truth is like the sun. You can shut it out for a
time, but it's not going to go away.
—*Elvis Presley*

Truth is such a rare thing, it is a delight to tell it.
—*Emily Dickinson*

Don't bend; don't water it down; don't try to make
it logical; don't edit your own soul according to
fashion. Rather, follow your most
intense obsessions mercilessly.
—*Franz Kafka*

I hope I shall possess firmness and virtue enough
to maintain what I consider the most enviable of

all titles, the character of an honest man.
—*President, George Washington*

Almost any difficulty will move in the face of
honesty. When I am honest I never feel stupid.
And when I am honest I am automatically humble.
—*Hugh Prather*

All men profess honesty as long as they can.
To believe all men honest would be folly.
To believe none so is something worse.
—*President, John Quincy Adams*

To make your children capable of honesty is the
beginning of education.
—*John Ruskin*

There are things to confess that enrich the world,
and things that need not be said.
—*Joni Mitchell*

Honesty is the rarest wealth anyone can possess,
and yet all the honesty in the world ain't lawful
tender for a loaf of bread.
—*Josh Billings*

And that's the thing about
people who mean everything they say.

They think everyone else does too.
—*Khaled Hosseini*

The real things haven't changed. It is best to be
honest and truthful; to make the most of what we
have; to be happy with simple pleasures; and have
courage when things go wrong.
—*Laura Ingalls Wilder*

Do not do what you would undo if caught.
—*Leah Arendt*

I have found that being honest is the best
technique I can use. Right up front, tell people
what you're trying to accomplish and what you're
willing to sacrifice to accomplish it.
—*Lee Iacocca*

The easiest thing to be in the world is you. The
most difficult thing to be is what other people
want you to be. Don't let them put
you in that position.
—*Leo Buscaglia*

If it is not right do not do it; if it is
not true do not say it.
—*Marcus Aurelius*

A lie can travel half way around the world while
the truth is putting on its shoes.
—*Mark Twain*

Honesty is the cornerstone of all success, without
which confidence and ability to perform
shall cease to exist.
—*Mary Kay Ash*

Let's tell the truth to people. When people ask,
'How are you?' have the nerve sometimes to
answer truthfully. You must know, however, that
people will start avoiding you because, they, too,
have knees that pain them and heads that hurt and
they don't want to know about yours. But think of
it this way: If people avoid you, you will have more
time to meditate and do fine research on a cure
for whatever truly afflicts you.
—*Maya Angelou*

The first thing is to be honest with yourself. You
can never have an impact on society if you have
not changed yourself. Great peacemakers are all
people of integrity, of honesty, but humility.
—*Nelson Mandela*

It's discouraging how many people are shocked by
honesty and how few by deceit.
—*Noel Coward*

Truth allows you to live with integrity. Everything
you do and say shows the world who you really
are. Let it be the truth.
—*Oprah Winfrey*

Never separate the life you lead from
the words you speak.
—*Paul Wellstone*

It takes two seconds to tell the truth and it costs
nothing. A lie takes time and [often]
costs everything.
—*Randi Rhodes*

Life demands honesty, the ability to face,
admit, and express oneself.
—*Starhawk*

We tell lies when we are afraid... afraid of what we
don't know, afraid of what others will think, afraid
of what will be found out about us.
But every time we tell a lie,
the thing that we fear grows stronger.
—*Tad Williams*

The only way you can truly control how you're
seen is by being honest all the time.
—*Tom Hanks*

Honesty is the first chapter in the book of wisdom.
—*Thomas Jefferson in a letter to Nathaniel Macon*

If you do not tell the truth about yourself you
cannot tell it about other people.
—*Virginia Woolf*

Honesty is a very expensive gift.
Do not expect it from cheap people.
—*Warren Buffet*

No legacy is so rich as honesty.
—*William Shakespeare*

Truth is incontrovertible, malice may attack it and
ignorance may deride it, but, in the end, there it is.
—*Sir Winston Churchill*

A half-truth is a whole lie.
—*Yiddish Proverb*

Honesty and integrity are absolutely essential for
success in life—all areas of life. The really good
news is that anyone can develop
both honesty and integrity.
—*Zig Ziglar*

Anonymously…

If you want to ruin the truth—stretch it.

Honesty will be provided to the
extent it is demanded.

Look a man in the eye and say what you really
think, don't just smile at him and say what
you're supposed to think.

If you truly want honesty, don't ask questions you
don't really want the answer to.

The cruelest lies are often unspoken.

Inconvenient facts are often the most useful and
the most difficult to share.

The truth needs no rehearsal.

If it is not right don't do it; if it is not true,
don't say it.

Honesty is the first chapter in the book of wisdom.[19]

Sometimes the truth hurts but never worse than a lie.

And from the author...

Let's be honest, honesty is not always being
honest with others, most often it is being
honest with ourselves.

If we choose to play by our own rules and bend
the truth, we will eventually be governed
by the rules of others.

I've never met an honest man
who had no friends.

What is it that makes some men liars when the cost
of the words which comprise the truth
are so inexpensive?

The question, *what will happen if I tell the truth*, is an
admission disguised as a lie, and the answer, *if I did,
it was a mistake*, is a lie disguised as an admission.

Next to a faithful dog, honesty is often a
man's best friend.

Sadly, when someone prefaces a statement with, *to*

be honest with you, that which follows is often
neither honest nor sincere.

The true measure of one's success in life is not the
accumulation of wealth, but the number of friends
that believe us to be honest.

*A Goatherd had sought to bring back a stray goat to his flock. He
whistled and sounded his horn in vain; the straggler paid no attention to the
summons. At last the Goatherd threw a large stone, and breaking its horn,
begged the Goat not to tell his master. The Goat replied, "Why, you
silly fellow, the horn will speak though I be silent."*[20]

Ernest Griset, 1874

Moral: Do not attempt to hide things which cannot be hid.

[19] This quote is often attributed to Thomas Jefferson. However, numerous others have claimed it to be theirs. Thus the author cites it, anonymous.

[20] Adopted from Townsend's version of Aesop's Fable, *The Goat and The Goatherd*. Aesop, a slave and story-teller, believed to have lived in ancient Greece between 620 and 560 BC. The stories associated with Aesop's name have traversed time. Aesop's collection of fables are collectively called, *Aesopica*, and are still enjoyed the world over.

10 CHARITY

Charity isn't about doling out grand amounts of money,
the receipt of accolades, or admiration from our peers.
Charity is withdrawing judgment and accepting that others
have differences, weaknesses, and shortcomings. Charity is
the refusal to take advantage of another's weaknesses and
vulnerabilities for personal gain or opportunity, but to see
their need and fill it. Charity is doing what you can,
when you can, for no reason other than you can.

G rowing up on a farm in Bettendorf, Iowa, Lillian was able to understand the plight of getting by with little. "We went without a lot of things because we simply couldn't afford them," she said sometime later. She was not alone. Many a dirt farmer in Eastern Iowa shared her misery. "We did so much with so little for so long, it seemed we could do anything with nothing, forever," said a neighbor. To help the family, Lillian's mother taught her to sew before the age of ten. Later, out of necessity, as a mother of five herself, she used her meager skills to clothe her entire family.

Then several years ago, Lillian discovered a Christian nonprofit called Little Dresses for Africa. Without a second thought, she realized instantly she could help. She told a friend, "These little girls, I can imagine that they have a lot of feelings, maybe even worse than what we had to go through." She immediately went to work. Using her sewing skills she began to sew and make a one-of-a-kind dress for a little girl in Africa that she will never meet. She then sewed another and another. Each dress took about four hours from start to finish.

Her sewing became an obsession. "I don't even watch television," she told NBC news reporter. "My dresses became my entertainment [and my purpose]," she said. At last count, she has made over 900 unique and personalized dresses. "I think that it's very important to have something different for these little girls…I imagine four or five of them standing in a row and they got a little dress on and they're all different."

Rachel O'Neill, founder and director of Little Dresses for Africa, says that Lillian is her personal hero. "I never get tired of looking at them," O'Neill said about the dresses "She likes to do the little extra and believe me, [the young girls] love it." To O'Neill's credit, and the charity of others like Lillian who love to sew, Little Dresses has now distributed over 2.5 million dresses to 81 different countries.

Lillian's big heart and able hands are certainly special, but what makes her story extraordinary is that in 2015, Lillian will turn 100 years old. Her goal is to make 1,000 dresses by her 100th birthday. "It keeps me going after 99 years," she claims. "I don't know what I would have done if I hadn't found this to do. I have been blessed." Despite her 100th birthday approaching, Lillian has no intention of slowing down. "If I'm still able to do it I'll continue all the way through because I know I'm making little girls happy, [and that has become my purpose]."

Lillian Webster is a *hero*. She saw a need she could fill and filled it. She did not allow her age, her circumstances, or past impede her desire to help. At the age of 99, Lilian Webster recognized that charity is indeed, doing what *you can*, when you can, for no reason other than you can. In doing so, she delivered happiness, comfort, and pride to hundreds of little girls in Africa.

What we do for ourselves dies with us. What we do
for others and the world remains
and is immortal.
—*Albert Pine*

No one has ever become poor by giving.
—*Anne Frank*

It is not what we get, but who we become, what
we contribute…that gives meaning to our lives.
—*Anthony Robbins*

Charity never humiliated him who profited from it,
nor ever bound him by the chains of

gratitude, since it was not to him but to
God that the gift was made.
— *Antoine de Saint-Exupéry*

Remember, if you ever need a helping hand, you'll
find one at the end of your arm...As you grow
older you will discover that you have two hands.
One for helping yourself, the other
for helping others.
—*Aubrey Hepburn*

Blessed are those who give without remembering.
And blessed are those who take without forgetting.
—*Bernard Meltzer*

If you haven't got any charity in your heart, you
have the worst kind of heart trouble.
—*Bob Hope*

No person was ever honored for what he received.
Honor has been the reward for what he gave.
—*President, Calvin Coolidge*

No one is useless in this world who lightens
the burden of another.
—*Charles Dickens*

Nothing brings me more happiness than trying to
help the most vulnerable people in society.

It is a goal and an essential part
of my life—a kind of destiny.
—*Princess Diana Frances Mountbatten-Windsor*

The human contribution is the essential ingredient.
It is only in the giving of oneself
to others that we truly live.
—*Ethel Percy Andrus*

Flatter not thyself in thy faith in God if thou hast
not charity for thy neighbor.
—*Francis Quarles*

When you stop [providing value] to the rest of the
world, it's time to turn out the lights.
—*George Burns*

Let your heart feel for the afflictions and distresses
of every one, and let your hand give in proportion
to your purse; remembering always the estimation
of the widow's mite, but, that it is not every
one who asketh that deserveth charity; all,
however, are worthy of the inquiry,
or the deserving may suffer.
—*President, George Washington*

Charity sees the need, not the cause.
—*German Proverb*

A rich man without charity is a rogue; and perhaps
it would be no difficult a matter to
prove that he is also a fool.
—*Henry Fielding*

The life of a man consists not in seeing visions and
in dreaming dreams, but in active charity
and in willing service.
—*Henry Wadsworth Longfellow*

Do not give, as many rich men do, like a hen that
lays her egg and then cackles.
—*Henry Ward Beecher*

The highest exercise of charity is charity
towards the uncharitable.
—*Jonathan Swift*

A bone to the dog is not charity. Charity is the
bone shared with the dog, when you are
just as hungry as the dog.
—*Jack London*

You have not lived today until you have done
something for someone who can never repay you.
—*John Bunyon*

There is no exercise better for the heart than
reaching down and lifting people up.
—*John Holmes*

Nothing is so hard for those who abound in riches
to conceive how others can be in want.
—*Jonathan Swift*

You give but little when you give of your
possessions. It is when you give of
yourself that you truly give.
—*Kahlil Gibran*

An effort made for the happiness
of others lifts us above ourselves.
—*Lydia Maria Child*

The simplest acts of kindness are by far more
powerful than a thousand heads bowing in prayer.
—*Mahatma Gandhi*

Never doubt that a small group of concerned
citizens can change the world. Indeed,
it is the only thing that ever has.
—*Margaret Mead*

One must know not just how to accept a gift,
but with what grace to share it.
—*Maya Angelou*

The way you get meaning into your life is to
devote yourself to loving others, devote yourself to
your community around you, and devote yourself
to creating something that gives you
purpose and meaning.
—*Mitch Albom*

It is not how much we give but how much
love we put into giving.
—*Mother Teresa*

The true meaning of life is to plant trees, under
whose shade you do not expect to sit.
—*Nelson Henderson*

It is possible to give without loving, but it is
impossible to love without giving.
—*Richard Braunstein*

The gifts that one receives for giving are so
immeasurable that it is almost
an injustice to accept them.
—*Rod McKeun*

He who waits to do a great deal of good at
once will never do anything.
—*Samuel Johnson*

Be charitable before wealth makes you covetous.
—*Sir Thomas Browne*

The great use of life is to spend it for
something that outlasts it.
—*William James*

If there is any kindness I can show, or any good
thing I can do to any fellow being, let me do it
now, and not deter or neglect it,
as I shall not pass this way again.
—*William Penn*

The best portion of a good man's life, his little,
nameless, unremembered acts
of kindness and love.
—*William Wordsworth*

Anonymously...

If you want to touch the past, touch a rock. If you
want to touch the present, touch a flower. If you
want to touch the future, touch a life.

I am only one. But still I am one. I cannot do
everything, but still I can do something. And

because I cannot do everything, I will not refuse to
do the something that I can do.

Dream what you want to dream; go where you
want to go; be what you want to be; because you
have only one life to live and one chance to do all
the things that need to be done.

The charitable give out the door and God puts it
back through the window.

The character of a people [is often]
ruined by charity.

And from the author...

If the world seems cold to you, do something
kind to warm it.

Charity is not about giving, it is knowing
when to give.

When you are looking for obstacles, you won't
find opportunities to give.

A man's priorities and values are evidenced by
his credit card statement.

As iron is eaten by rust, the envious are
consumed by greed.

Give people more than they expect
and do it cheerfully.

It may seem odd, but the more I give,
the more I receive.

Andrew Carnegie was a Scottish-American industrialist who, among others, led the enormous expansion of America's steel industry in the late 19th century. He was also one of America's greatest philanthropists. By 1919 he had given away almost 90 percent of his fortune to charities and foundations.[21] In an 1889 article entitled, *The Gospel of Wealth* he called on the rich to use their wealth to improve society and the condition of man. In that piece he offered this advice:

"In bestowing charity, the main consideration: should be to help those who will help themselves; to provide part of the means by which those who desire to improve may do so; to give those who desire to rise the aids by which they may rise; to assist, but rarely or never to do all. Neither the individual nor the race is improved by aims-giving. Those worthy of assistance, except in rare cases, seldom require assistance. The really valuable men of the race never do, except in case of accident or sudden change. Everyone has of course, cases of individuals brought to his own knowledge where temporary assistance can do genuine good, and these he will not overlook. But the amount which can be wisely given by the individual for individuals is necessarily limited by his lack of knowledge of the circumstances connected with each. He is the only true reformer who is

as careful and as anxious not to aid the unworthy as he is to aid the worthy, and, perhaps, even more so, for in aims-giving more injury is probably done by rewarding vice than by relieving virtue."

Andrew Carnegie, 1913

[21] At the time of his death in 1919, Andrew Carnegie had made charitable contributions of over $350 million; the equivalent of $4.76 billion today. After the sale of his company, Carnegie Steel Company to J.P. Morgan in 1901, Carnegie devoted the remainder of his life to large-scale philanthropic undertaking, with special emphasis on local libraries, world peace, education and scientific research.

AFTERWORD

It is widely held that the human spirit is the incorporeal or ethereal part of man. It includes our intellect, emotions, fears, passions, and creativity. Of all other living things, it provides us and only us, the ability to imagine and reflect. According to Genesis 2:7, the source of this remarkable power is the *breath of God*. It makes each of us an example of what is possible, while granting us the ability to inspire greatness in others. Therefore, our greatest contribution to those around us is in large part, our own excellence. This book is about such people and their contribution. Eternally, they include:

Scott B. Crane, July 25, 1987—June 11, 2011

Edwin A. Shuman III, October 7, 1931—December 3, 2013

Constance S. Beneduci, April 8, 1907—June 30, 2001

Dr. Raymond S. Krug, September 9, 1933—April 15, 2009

Edward W. Sheehan, September 5, 1937—March 25, 2014

Jean Bell Mosley, September 21, 1913—July 11, 2003

Andrew Carnegie, November 25, 1835—August 11, 1919

I thank them. I also thank you, the reader, for taking the time to read this book. If you liked it, I am hopeful you will share it with others. In that spirit of sharing, the author, together with his publisher, AuthorVista LLC proudly donates a portion of the revenue from every book sold to these worthy organizations and others:

You can assist in this effort by sharing with me your inspiring quotes, quips, and virtue related stories. For editorial purposes I have created an extensive database of such. Any material that might be provided to us can be quickly compared to that which we have. If new and appropriate, we will happily use it in the future where possible, and of course attribute it accordingly.

When I stand before God at the end of my life,
I would hope that I would not have a single
bit of talent left, and I could say,
'I used everything you gave me.'
—Erma Bombeck

SPECIAL OFFERS

BUY 2 BOOKS AND GET 1 FREE

 Did you like this book? For a limited time only, for readers who purchase two copies, we'll ship them with another copy free! That's right, three copies of this book for the price of two. For details visit www.AuthorVista.com, click Store and use Promo Code: **FREEBOOK**. A nominal shipping charge will be added at checkout. This offer is not available for books purchased through Amazon.com.

SPECIAL GIFT OFFER

Want a special gift for that special someone? Then order them an author autographed copy of this wonderful book. The purchaser can request a personal message of 25 words or less for that special someone, handwritten by the author above his autograph. For details visit www.AuthorVista.com, click Store and use Promo Code: **AUTOGRAPH**. This special offer is not available for books purchased through Amazon.com.

CUSTOMIZED VERSIONS OF THIS BOOK ARE AVAILABLE

Good books are powerful marketing tools. A well-written, creative book is capable of promoting a product, idea, service, or organization for the *author* who wrote it. AuthorVista can make you that *author*. Using its services, this book can be customized allowing the *author* (or an organization) to change the cover, add content or reorganize the entire book. So whether you need a corporate gift, a unique fundraising tool, and/or unique promotional vehicle, the hard work is already done. To learn more, visit AuthorVista.com or call 303.816.1636 today.

About the Author

 Eugene F. Ferraro, is a prolific writer and the author of more than 15 books, and hundreds of articles. He has been involved in the study of organizational culture, workplace investigations, and compliance for over 32 years. He is board certified in both Security Management and Human Resources Management (CPP and SPHR designations respectively). He frequently speaks and trains on the topics of writing, publishing, workplace misconduct, virtuosity, and organizational ethics. He is a former U.S. Marine Corps pilot, combat flight instructor, and a graduate of the Naval Justice School. He holds a Bachelor of Science degree from Florida Institute of Technology and is currently the Chief Ethics Officer of a global technology company based in Denver, Colorado.

Gene is also an outdoorsman, fly fisherman, extreme hiker, and rancher. He lives with his wife and their four magnificent horses in the mountains of Colorado. Those wishing to reach him are welcome to do so via email at Gene.Ferraro@AuthorVista.com.